Proven Social Media Business Strategies 2024

Unlock Growth, Build Engagement, and Amplify Your Brand Presence in the Social Media Sphere

Isabelle Sterling

Table of content

Chapter 1
Introduction

In the dynamic landscape of modern business, the role of social media has evolved from a mere communication platform to a powerful catalyst for growth and brand influence. This paradigm shift necessitates a nuanced understanding of social media business strategies to navigate the complexities of the digital realm effectively. As businesses strive to connect with their target audiences and establish a formidable online presence, a comprehensive approach to social media becomes paramount.

This introduction seeks to unravel the significance of leveraging social media for business success. In an era where consumer interactions, brand loyalty, and market trends are intricately woven into the fabric of online platforms, businesses must not only participate but excel in the digital conversation. The multifaceted nature of social media demands strategic foresight, adaptability, and an acute awareness of the diverse channels available.

As we embark on this exploration of social media business strategies, our journey begins with the fundamental understanding of the audience. Recognizing the demographic nuances, preferences, and behaviors of our target market lays the groundwork for tailored and effective communication. Subsequently, we delve into the meticulous crafting of a social media plan, defining clear objectives and selecting platforms that align with business goals.

The concept of building a strong brand presence emerges as a cornerstone, emphasizing the importance of consistent messaging and compelling visuals. Engaging content creation takes center stage, exploring the various mediums and techniques to captivate audiences. Community building and management become pivotal, transforming casual observers into loyal brand advocates.

Through this comprehensive guide, businesses will navigate the intricacies of paid advertising, analytics, and crisis management, culminating in the ability to measure success and return on investment. Join us as we unravel the layers of social media strategies, providing insights and practical approaches to empower businesses in the ever-evolving digital landscape.

The Importance of Social Media for Business

In the contemporary business landscape, the importance of social media cannot be overstated. Social media platforms have transcended their initial role as mere communication channels and have emerged as indispensable tools for businesses aiming to thrive in a digitally interconnected world.

At the heart of social media's significance lies its unparalleled ability to connect businesses with their target audiences. These platforms serve as dynamic hubs where consumers not only seek information but actively engage with brands. Establishing a robust presence on popular social media channels allows businesses to tap into a global pool of potential customers, fostering brand awareness and creating avenues for meaningful interactions.

Moreover, social media platforms provide a unique space for businesses to showcase their brand personality. Through compelling storytelling, visually appealing content, and authentic engagement, companies can shape their identity and build a loyal following. This direct interaction with the audience humanizes the brand, creating a sense of connection that extends beyond traditional marketing approaches.

In addition to being a powerful branding tool, social media serves as an effective means of market research. Businesses can gain valuable insights into consumer behavior, preferences, and emerging trends by monitoring conversations and engagement metrics. This real-time feedback loop empowers companies to adapt swiftly to changing market dynamics and tailor their strategies to meet evolving consumer expectations.

The viral nature of social media amplifies the reach of content, enabling businesses to extend their influence far beyond traditional marketing channels. A well-crafted post or campaign has the potential to go viral, exponentially increasing brand visibility and attracting new customers.

Ultimately, the importance of social media for business lies in its transformative capacity to level the playing field. Whether a startup or an established enterprise, a strategic and authentic presence on social media can propel a business to new heights, fostering growth, customer loyalty, and sustained success in the digital age.

Chapter 2
Understanding Your Audience

Understanding your audience is the cornerstone of effective social media strategy. In the intricate web of digital interactions, businesses that grasp the nuances of their target demographic gain a competitive edge. This understanding goes beyond basic demographics, delving into the behavioral patterns, preferences, and aspirations of the audience.

Demographic analysis forms the initial layer of comprehension. Identifying factors such as age, gender, location, and income levels provides a foundational understanding of who comprises the audience. However, a deeper exploration is essential. What are their interests? How do they consume content? What challenges do they face? Answering these questions facilitates the creation of content that resonates on a personal level.

Behavior and preferences lie at the heart of audience understanding. Monitoring online behaviors helps businesses tailor content and engagement strategies. Recognizing the preferred social media platforms, the type of content they engage with, and the frequency of their interactions enables a more targeted approach. This insight allows businesses to allocate resources effectively, focusing on platforms and content formats that yield the highest engagement.

Competitor analysis adds another layer to audience understanding. By evaluating the social media strategies of competitors, businesses can identify gaps and opportunities in the market. This not only informs strategic decisions but also aids in differentiating the brand by offering unique value propositions that address unmet needs within the target audience.

In essence, understanding your audience goes beyond surface-level demographics, evolving into a comprehensive grasp of their behaviors, preferences, and the broader market landscape. Armed with this knowledge, businesses can craft compelling content, tailor communication strategies, and build authentic connections that resonate with their audience on a profound level. This strategic alignment lays the foundation for sustained engagement, loyalty, and ultimately, business success in the ever-evolving digital landscape.

Demographic Analysis

Demographic analysis is a pivotal component of understanding your audience in the realm of social media. It involves examining and interpreting statistical data related to the characteristics of a population, offering valuable insights for businesses seeking to tailor their strategies to specific groups.

1. **Age:**
- Understanding the age distribution of your audience helps shape content and tone. For example, younger demographics may respond

well to trendier content, while older audiences might prefer more classic and informative material.

2. **Gender:**
- Gender analysis assists in crafting messages that resonate with different gender identities. This awareness ensures that marketing efforts are inclusive and considerate of diverse perspectives.

3. **Location:**
- Geographic data is crucial for localized targeting. Knowing where your audience is concentrated enables businesses to tailor promotions, events, or content to specific regions, optimizing relevance.

4. **Income Levels:**
- Recognizing the income levels of your audience aids in pricing strategies and product positioning. It also helps determine the type of promotions or discounts that would be most appealing.

5. **Education:**
- Understanding the educational background of your audience informs the complexity of your messaging. Highly educated audiences may appreciate in-depth content, while simpler messaging might be more suitable for others.

6. **Occupation:**
- Knowing the professional backgrounds of your audience allows for targeted B2B marketing and the creation of content that aligns with their industry interests and needs.

7. **Family Status:**
- Whether your audience consists of singles, families, or empty nesters influences the types of products or services they might be interested in. This knowledge guides marketing efforts toward relevant offerings.

8. **Interests and Hobbies:**
- Analyzing the hobbies and interests of your audience contributes to content creation.

Aligning your content with their passions enhances engagement and builds a sense of community around your brand.

Demographic analysis serves as a compass, guiding businesses toward a more nuanced understanding of their audience. By interpreting and acting upon this data, businesses can tailor their social media approach, ensuring that their content resonates authentically with the specific demographics they aim to reach.

Behavior and Preferences

Behavior and preferences play a pivotal role in shaping effective social media strategies. Understanding how your audience behaves on digital platforms and their preferences in terms of content consumption is essential for creating engaging and relevant interactions.

1. **Content Consumption Habits:**
   - Analyzing how your audience consumes content—whether they prefer short videos,

long-form articles, infographics, or interactive posts—guides the creation of content that aligns with their preferred formats.

2. **Browsing Patterns:**
- Recognizing how users navigate social media platforms provides insights into their attention spans and the optimal timing for posting content. This information ensures that your content is more likely to be seen and engaged with.

3. **Engagement Levels:**
- Monitoring the types of posts that receive high engagement (likes, comments, shares) helps identify what resonates most with your audience. This insight can be leveraged to replicate successful content strategies.

4. **Shopping Behavior:**
- Understanding how your audience approaches online shopping, including the factors influencing their purchasing decisions, allows for more targeted and effective e-commerce strategies.

5. **Interactions with Brands:**
- Examining how your audience engages with other brands on social media provides valuable competitive insights. It helps in crafting a strategy that differentiates your brand and meets or exceeds audience expectations.

6. **Response to Trends:**
- Observing how your audience responds to trends and cultural movements enables businesses to align their content with popular themes, fostering relatability and connection.

7. **Platform Preferences:**
- Identifying the social media platforms your audience frequents allows for focused efforts on the channels most likely to reach and engage them effectively.

8. **Feedback and Reviews:**
- Paying attention to audience feedback and reviews provides a direct line to their preferences and concerns. This information is

instrumental in refining products, services, and overall brand perception.

By delving into the behavioral patterns and preferences of your audience, businesses can tailor their social media content and engagement strategies to meet the specific needs and expectations of their target demographic. This personalized approach fosters stronger connections, higher engagement levels, and ultimately contributes to the overall success of a social media campaign.

Competitor Analysis

Competitor analysis in the realm of social media is a strategic process that involves evaluating the strengths and weaknesses of rivals within the same industry. By examining their social media presence, content strategies, and engagement tactics, businesses can glean valuable insights to refine their own approach and gain a competitive edge.

1. **Social Media Platforms:**
- Identify the platforms where your competitors maintain a strong presence. Assess the reasons behind their platform choices and the effectiveness of their strategies on each.

2. **Audience Engagement:**
- Analyze how well your competitors engage with their audience. This includes the frequency and quality of their interactions, response time, and the level of community building achieved.

3. **Content Strategies:**
- Evaluate the types of content your competitors share. Determine the themes, formats, and frequency of their posts. Identify the content that generates the most engagement and the strategies they employ for storytelling.

4. **Branding and Messaging:**
- Examine the consistency of your competitors' branding across different social media channels. Assess their messaging tone, brand personality, and the emotions they evoke in their audience.

5. **Follower Growth:**
- Track the growth of your competitors' follower base. Understand the tactics they use to attract and retain followers, including any promotional campaigns or collaborations that contribute to their growth.

6. **Promotional Activities:**
- Investigate the promotions and campaigns your competitors run on social media. Assess the effectiveness of their promotions, the use of hashtags, and the integration of user-generated content.

7. **Innovative Approaches:**
- Identify any innovative or unique approaches your competitors employ. This includes interactive features, live videos, or any emerging trends they leverage to stay ahead in the social media landscape.

8. **Customer Feedback:**

- Examine customer feedback on your competitors' social media channels. Understand the sentiment, common concerns, and areas where they excel. This information can help refine your own customer engagement strategy.

By conducting a thorough competitor analysis, businesses can not only stay informed about industry trends but also discover opportunities for differentiation. Leveraging insights gained from competitors can guide the development of a more effective and distinctive social media strategy, ultimately positioning a business to better meet the expectations of its target audience.

Chapter 3
Crafting a Solid Social Media Plan

Crafting a solid social media plan is a strategic process that involves defining clear objectives, selecting the right platforms, and developing a well-structured content calendar. Here's a step-by-step guide to help businesses establish a robust social media strategy:

1. **Set Clear Objectives:**
- Define specific, measurable, achievable, relevant, and time-bound (SMART) objectives for your social media efforts. Whether it's increasing brand awareness, driving website traffic, or boosting sales, clarity in objectives is crucial.

2. **Know Your Target Audience:**
- Leverage the insights gained from demographic and behavioral analysis to identify and understand your target audience. Tailor your

content to resonate with their preferences, interests, and needs.

3. **Choose the Right Platforms:**
- Select social media platforms that align with your business goals and where your target audience is most active. Each platform has its own strengths, so choose strategically based on your content and communication style.

4. **Content Calendar and Scheduling:**
- Develop a content calendar outlining the frequency and timing of your posts. Plan a mix of content types, including educational, entertaining, and promotional posts. Use scheduling tools to maintain consistency.

5. **Content Creation Guidelines:**
- Establish branding and content creation guidelines to ensure consistency across all social media channels. Define your brand voice, visual elements, and messaging style to create a cohesive online identity.

6. **Engagement Strategy:**
- Outline how you will engage with your audience. Respond promptly to comments, messages, and mentions. Consider running polls, Q&A sessions, or contests to encourage interaction.

7. **Monitoring and Analytics:**
- Implement tools to monitor social media analytics. Track key metrics such as reach, engagement, and conversions. Regularly analyze the data to understand what works and refine your strategy accordingly.

8. **Paid Advertising Strategy:**
- If budget allows, consider incorporating paid advertising into your social media plan. Define your target audience, set a budget, and create compelling ad creatives. Monitor and adjust your campaigns based on performance.

9. **Collaborations and Partnerships:**
- Explore opportunities for collaborations and partnerships with influencers or other businesses

in your industry. Strategic alliances can extend your reach and introduce your brand to new audiences.

10. **Adaptability and Evolution:**
- Social media trends are dynamic. Be adaptable and ready to evolve your strategy based on platform updates, changes in user behavior, and emerging trends. Stay informed and continuously optimize your approach.

By following these steps and continually refining your social media plan, businesses can establish a strong online presence, foster engagement, and achieve their overarching objectives in the ever-evolving landscape of social media.

Setting Clear Objectives

Setting clear objectives is the foundation of a successful social media strategy. Here's a guide to help businesses define objectives that are specific, measurable, achievable, relevant, and time-bound (SMART):

1. **Specific:**
- Clearly define what you want to achieve. Instead of a broad goal like "increase brand awareness," specify the aspect of awareness you aim to enhance, such as increasing mentions or improving recognition among a particular demographic.

2. **Measurable:**
- Establish metrics to quantify your objectives. Whether it's increasing followers, engagement rates, website traffic, or sales, having measurable indicators enables you to track progress and assess the success of your social media efforts.

3. **Achievable:**
- Ensure that your objectives are realistic and attainable within your resources and constraints. Setting overly ambitious goals may lead to frustration, while realistic targets foster motivation and a sense of accomplishment.

4. **Relevant:**
- Align your social media objectives with broader business goals. Consider how achieving these objectives contributes to overall success. For instance, if the goal is to increase online sales, social media efforts could focus on driving traffic to the e-commerce platform.

5. **Time-Bound:**
- Set specific timeframes for achieving your objectives. Whether it's a short-term goal like increasing engagement within a month or a long-term goal like doubling followers over a year, having deadlines adds urgency and helps in planning.

Example of SMART Objectives:
- **Specific:** Increase brand mentions on social media by 20%.
- **Measurable:** Track the number of mentions using social media monitoring tools.
- **Achievable:** Allocate resources for social listening tools and engagement strategies.

- **Relevant:** Enhance brand visibility and perception, contributing to overall marketing goals.
- **Time-Bound:** Achieve the 20% increase in brand mentions within the next three months.

By adhering to the SMART framework, businesses can create objectives that provide clarity, focus, and a roadmap for success in their social media endeavors. Regularly revisiting and adjusting these objectives ensures that the social media strategy remains aligned with evolving business priorities.

Choosing the Right Platforms

Choosing the right social media platforms is crucial for an effective strategy. Consider the following steps to identify platforms that align with your business goals and target audience:

1. **Understand Your Audience:**
- Refer to demographic and behavioral analysis to identify the social media platforms where

your target audience is most active. Different demographics favor specific platforms, so understanding this is key.

2. **Align with Business Goals:**
- Match the features of each platform with your business objectives. For example, if visual content is essential, platforms like Instagram or Pinterest may be more suitable, while LinkedIn might be preferable for B2B networking.

3. **Evaluate Platform Strengths:**
- Each platform has unique strengths. Facebook is versatile for various content types, Twitter is ideal for real-time updates, Instagram is visual-centric, LinkedIn is business-focused, and TikTok is popular for short-form videos. Assess these strengths against your content strategy.

4. **Consider Industry Trends:**
- Stay informed about emerging trends in social media usage. New platforms may gain popularity, or existing ones may evolve. Being

aware of these trends helps you adapt and explore new opportunities.

5. **Resource Allocation:**
- Consider the resources required to maintain an active presence on each platform. If your team has limitations, focus on platforms that align with your priorities and where you can consistently produce quality content.

6. **Competitor Presence:**
- Analyze where your competitors are active. While you shouldn't replicate their strategy, understanding where they engage successfully can provide insights into platform effectiveness within your industry.

7. **User Engagement Metrics:**
- Review the engagement metrics of your current social media channels. Platforms where you already have an audience or see higher engagement may be worth prioritizing.

8. **Test and Evaluate:**

- Experiment with multiple platforms initially, but be ready to refine your strategy based on performance. Track metrics such as engagement rates, follower growth, and conversion rates to assess platform effectiveness.

9. **Audience Preferences:**
- Understand the content preferences of your target audience. Some audiences prefer informative articles on LinkedIn, while others may engage more with visual content on Instagram. Tailor your platform choices to these preferences.

10. **Adaptability:**
- Be adaptable to changes in platform popularity and functionality. Social media evolves, and being flexible allows you to capitalize on new opportunities and adjust your strategy accordingly.

By carefully considering these factors, businesses can make informed decisions about the social media platforms that best serve their objectives and audience, optimizing their efforts for maximum impact.

Content Calendar and Scheduling

Creating a content calendar and implementing a scheduling strategy is essential for maintaining consistency and effectiveness in your social media efforts. Here's a step-by-step guide to help you establish a content calendar:

1. **Define Your Content Mix:**
- Determine the types of content you want to share, such as blog posts, images, videos, polls, or user-generated content. A diverse content mix keeps your audience engaged.

2. **Understand Your Audience's Habits:**
- Refer to behavioral analysis to identify the times and days when your audience is most active on social media. Tailor your posting schedule to maximize visibility during peak engagement periods.

3. **Establish Content Themes:**
- Plan content themes for specific days or weeks. This provides a structure for your calendar and helps align your content with campaigns, seasons, or relevant industry events.

4. **Assign Responsibilities:**
- If you have a team, assign responsibilities for content creation, approval, and scheduling. Clearly define roles to ensure a seamless workflow and timely content delivery.

5. **Use a Content Calendar Tool:**
- Utilize tools like content management platforms or social media scheduling tools (e.g., Hootsuite, Buffer) to plan and schedule posts in advance. These tools streamline the process and offer analytics for performance tracking.

6. **Incorporate Hashtags and Keywords:**
- Include relevant hashtags and keywords in your content calendar to increase discoverability. Research popular and industry-specific hashtags to enhance your content's visibility.

7. **Plan Campaigns and Promotions:**
- If you have upcoming campaigns, product launches, or promotions, integrate them into your content calendar. Ensure that your social media posts align with these initiatives to create a cohesive marketing strategy.

8. **Balance Promotional and Engaging Content:**
- Maintain a balance between promotional content and engaging, informative posts. Too much promotion can alienate your audience, so intersperse it with content that provides value or entertains.

9. **Monitor Trends and Relevance:**
- Stay informed about current events, trends, and industry news. Adjust your content calendar to reflect timely and relevant topics, demonstrating your brand's adaptability and awareness.

10. **Evaluate and Adjust:**

- Regularly review the performance of your posts and overall engagement. Use analytics tools to assess what works well and what needs improvement. Adjust your content calendar based on these insights.

By following these steps, businesses can develop a well-organized content calendar that ensures a consistent and strategic presence on social media. This proactive approach not only saves time but also enhances the impact of your social media content.

Chapter 4
Building a Strong Brand Presence

Building a strong brand presence on social media is essential for creating lasting impressions and fostering connections with your audience. Here's a guide to help businesses establish and enhance their brand presence:

1. **Define Your Brand Identity:**
- Clearly articulate your brand values, mission, and personality. Ensure consistency in how your brand is presented across all social media channels.

2. **Create a Cohesive Visual Branding:**
- Use consistent colors, fonts, and imagery to create a visual identity that reflects your brand. This visual consistency helps in instant brand recognition.

3. **Craft a Compelling Bio:**

- Write a concise and compelling bio that encapsulates your brand essence. Use keywords relevant to your industry to enhance discoverability.

4. **Share Authentic Content:**
- Develop content that resonates with your audience and aligns with your brand voice. Authenticity builds trust and fosters a genuine connection with your followers.

5. **Tell Your Brand Story:**
- Share the story behind your brand. Highlight milestones, values, and the people behind the scenes. A compelling narrative creates an emotional connection with your audience.

6. **Consistent Posting Schedule:**
- Maintain a consistent posting schedule to keep your brand top-of-mind. Regular, predictable content delivery reinforces your brand presence in the minds of your audience.

7. **Engage with Your Audience:**

- Respond promptly to comments, messages, and mentions. Engage in conversations with your audience to humanize your brand and build a community around it.

8. **Utilize Brand Hashtags:**
- Create and promote branded hashtags. Encourage your audience to use them, fostering a sense of community and enabling easy tracking of user-generated content related to your brand.

9. **Showcase User-Generated Content:**
- Share content created by your audience. This not only recognizes and appreciates your community but also provides authentic social proof of your brand's value.

10. **Collaborate with Influencers:**
- Partner with influencers or thought leaders in your industry. Their endorsement can amplify your brand's reach and credibility.

11. **Host Branded Events or Challenges:**

- Organize online events, challenges, or contests aligned with your brand values. Encourage participation and create a buzz around your brand.

12. **Monitor Brand Mentions:**
- Regularly monitor mentions of your brand on social media. Respond to both positive and negative mentions promptly, showing that you are attentive and value customer feedback.

13. **Measure Brand Metrics:**
- Use analytics tools to measure brand-related metrics, such as brand mentions, sentiment, and follower growth. Analyze the data to refine your brand strategy.

By systematically implementing these strategies, businesses can establish a strong and memorable brand presence on social media, contributing to increased brand loyalty and recognition in the digital space.

Branding Guidelines for Social Media

Creating consistent branding guidelines for social media is crucial to present a unified and recognizable brand image across various platforms. Here's a comprehensive guide to establishing effective branding guidelines:

1. **Define Brand Elements:**
- Clearly outline your brand elements, including logo variations, color palette, typography, and imagery style. These elements form the visual foundation of your brand.

2. **Logo Usage:**
- Specify guidelines for the correct usage of your logo. Include size requirements, clear space around the logo, and variations for different backgrounds or platforms.

3. **Color Palette:**
- Provide a defined color palette for your brand. Specify primary and secondary colors, as well as their Pantone, RGB, and Hex codes.

Ensure consistency in color application across all social media assets.

4. **Typography:**
- Select specific fonts for your brand and define their usage. Specify font styles for headings, body text, and any other typographic elements. Consistency in font usage enhances brand recognition.

5. **Imagery Style:**
- Describe the style of imagery that aligns with your brand. Specify the types of photos, illustrations, or graphics that convey the desired brand aesthetics. Consistent imagery creates a cohesive visual identity.

6. **Voice and Tone:**
- Define the brand voice and tone for social media communication. Whether it's casual, formal, or a mix, maintaining a consistent tone across platforms ensures a unified brand personality.

7. **Messaging Guidelines:**
- Outline key brand messages and taglines.
Provide guidance on how to convey your brand
story, values, and unique selling propositions in
a succinct and compelling manner.

8. **Social Media Platforms:**
- Tailor guidelines for each social media
platform. Consider platform-specific image
sizes, character limits, and any unique features
that may impact how your brand is presented.

9. **Profile Picture and Cover Photo
Guidelines:**
- Specify the dimensions and content for
profile pictures and cover photos on each
platform. Ensure that these images align with
your overall branding and convey a consistent
message.

10. **Use of Hashtags and Mentions:**
- Provide guidance on the use of branded
hashtags and mentions. Encourage consistent use

to enhance brand visibility and facilitate
community engagement.

11. **Response Protocol:**
- Establish a response protocol for engaging
with followers, handling comments, and
addressing inquiries or concerns. Consistency in
responses contributes to a trustworthy and
reliable brand image.

12. **Legal and Compliance Considerations:**
- Include any legal considerations related to
branding, such as copyright information,
disclaimers, or usage restrictions. Ensure
compliance with regulations governing your
industry.

13. **Periodic Review and Updates:**
- Schedule regular reviews of your branding
guidelines to ensure relevance and alignment
with evolving business goals. Update guidelines
as needed to reflect changes in brand strategy or
design trends.

By establishing and adhering to comprehensive branding guidelines, businesses can maintain a cohesive and recognizable brand presence on social media. This consistency contributes to brand trust, loyalty, and a strong visual identity in the digital space.

Consistent Messaging and Visuals

Consistent messaging and visuals are paramount for creating a cohesive and memorable brand identity on social media. Here's a guide to achieving consistency in both aspects:

Consistent Messaging:

1. **Define Brand Voice:**
- Clearly articulate your brand voice – the tone and style of communication. Whether it's friendly, professional, or humorous, maintain a consistent voice across all social media channels.

2. **Craft Core Messages:**

- Identify key brand messages that align with your values, mission, and unique selling propositions. These core messages should be consistently communicated across various social media posts.

3. **Maintain Tone Across Platforms:**
- Adapt your messaging for different platforms while preserving a consistent tone. The way you communicate on LinkedIn might differ from Twitter, but the overall brand tone should remain recognizable.

4. **Use Consistent Language:**
- Establish a set of preferred terms and language choices. Consistency in language enhances brand recognition and reinforces your brand's personality.

5. **Storytelling Guidelines:**
- Develop guidelines for brand storytelling. Whether it's sharing customer success stories, behind-the-scenes glimpses, or company

milestones, ensure that the storytelling approach aligns with your brand narrative.

6. **Incorporate Brand Taglines:**
- Integrate brand taglines or slogans consistently in your messaging. These succinct phrases contribute to brand recall and reinforce key brand attributes.

7. **Response Strategy:**
- Define a consistent strategy for responding to comments, mentions, and messages. Whether your brand adopts a friendly, informative, or problem-solving approach, maintain uniformity in responses.

Consistent Visuals:

1. **Establish Design Elements:**
- Define the core design elements, including color schemes, fonts, and graphic styles. Consistency in these elements contributes to a visually cohesive brand identity.

2. **Logo Usage Guidelines:**
- Clearly outline how your logo should be used in different contexts. Provide specifications for size, color variations, and placement to ensure uniformity.

3. **Color Palette:**
- Specify the primary and secondary colors that represent your brand. Ensure that these colors are consistently used in graphics, images, and other visual elements across social media platforms.

4. **Typography Standards:**
- Set guidelines for typography, including font choices for headlines, body text, and other text elements. Consistent typography enhances readability and brand recognition.

5. **Imagery Style:**
- Establish a cohesive style for imagery, whether it's photography, illustrations, or graphics. Consistency in style contributes to a unified visual language.

6. **Social Media Templates:**
- Create templates for social media graphics to maintain a consistent look and feel. These templates can be adapted for different types of content while preserving visual coherence.

7. **Profile Picture and Cover Photo:**
- Ensure that profile pictures and cover photos are consistently designed across different social media platforms. These visuals are often the first impression users have of your brand.

8. **Grid Aesthetics (if applicable):**
- If your brand follows a specific grid aesthetic on platforms like Instagram, provide guidelines for maintaining this visual continuity. Consistency in the overall feed enhances the visual appeal.

By rigorously adhering to guidelines for messaging and visuals, businesses can create a brand identity on social media that is not only visually appealing but also resonates with their target audience and reinforces key brand attributes.

Storytelling Techniques

Effective storytelling on social media is a powerful tool for engaging your audience, conveying your brand message, and building a lasting connection. Here are some storytelling techniques tailored for social media:

1. **Know Your Audience:**
- Understand your audience's preferences, interests, and pain points. Tailor your stories to resonate with their experiences and aspirations.

2. **Begin with a Hook:**
- Capture attention right away with a compelling hook. Whether it's a question, a surprising fact, or an intriguing statement, make your audience curious from the start.

3. **Create Relatable Characters:**

- Introduce relatable characters in your stories. This could be your team members, satisfied customers, or individuals who have benefited from your product or service. Humanizing your brand fosters a stronger connection.

4. **Show, Don't Just Tell:**
- Use visuals, such as images or short videos, to complement your storytelling. Visual content is highly engaging and can convey emotions and messages more effectively than text alone.

5. **Build Tension and Resolution:**
- Structure your stories with a narrative arc. Introduce a conflict or challenge, build tension, and then resolve it. This keeps your audience engaged and invested in the outcome.

6. **Use Authenticity:**
- Be authentic and transparent in your storytelling. Share real experiences, challenges, and successes. Authenticity resonates with audiences and builds trust.

7. **Incorporate User-Generated Content:**
   - Share stories from your customers or followers. User-generated content adds authenticity and diversity to your narrative, showcasing real experiences with your brand.

8. **Utilize Series or Themes:**
   - Create thematic series or story arcs. This encourages your audience to follow along for more, increasing engagement and creating a sense of continuity.

9. **Encourage Audience Participation:**
   - Foster interaction by asking questions or encouraging your audience to share their own stories. This not only enhances engagement but also makes your storytelling more interactive.

10. **Keep It Concise:**
   - Social media platforms often favor concise content. Craft stories that are succinct but impactful. If a longer narrative is needed, consider breaking it into digestible parts or using the swipe feature where applicable.

11. **Create a Brand Persona:**
- Develop a consistent brand persona that aligns with your storytelling. Whether it's playful, authoritative, or empathetic, maintain a consistent tone throughout your stories.

12. **Use Story Highlights:**
- Utilize features like story highlights on platforms like Instagram to curate and organize your stories. This allows followers to revisit key narratives or themes.

13. **Integrate Call-to-Action (CTA):**
- Conclude your stories with a clear call-to-action. This could be inviting users to share their thoughts, visit your website, or participate in a poll. Guide your audience on the next steps.

Remember, effective storytelling on social media is a blend of creativity, empathy, and strategic communication. Experiment with different techniques, analyze audience responses, and refine your storytelling approach based on what resonates best with your community.

Chapter 5
Engaging Content Creation

Engaging content creation is essential for capturing and maintaining the attention of your audience on social media. Here are some tips to help you create content that resonates and encourages interaction:

1. **Understand Your Audience:**

- Know your audience's preferences, interests, and behaviors. Tailor your content to align with what they find valuable and engaging.

2. **Visual Appeal:**
- Invest in visually appealing content. Use high-quality images, graphics, and videos to make your posts stand out. Visuals are often the first thing that grabs attention.

3. **Variety in Content Formats:**
- Diversify your content formats. Mix static images, carousels, videos, polls, and stories to keep your feed dynamic and cater to different content consumption preferences.

4. **Compelling Headlines:**
- Craft attention-grabbing headlines or captions. A compelling opening encourages users to read further or engage with your content.

5. **Tell Stories:**

- Incorporate storytelling techniques.
Narratives create emotional connections and
make your content more memorable.

6. **Educational Content:**
- Share informative and educational content.
How-to guides, tips, and industry insights
showcase your expertise and provide value to
your audience.

7. **User-Generated Content:**
- Feature user-generated content. Showcase
customer testimonials, reviews, or content
created by your audience. This not only provides
social proof but also encourages community
participation.

8. **Interactive Elements:**
- Include interactive elements like polls,
quizzes, and surveys. Encourage your audience
to participate, providing a sense of involvement
and making your content more shareable.

9. **Behind-the-Scenes Content:**

- Share behind-the-scenes glimpses of your business or team. Humanize your brand by letting your audience see the people and processes behind the products or services.

10. **Seasonal and Timely Content:**
- Create content that aligns with current events, seasons, or trends. Timely content shows that your brand is current and relevant.

11. **Incorporate Humor:**
- Use humor when appropriate. Humorous content tends to be shareable and can create a positive and memorable association with your brand.

12. **Embrace Trends and Challenges:**
- Participate in relevant social media trends or challenges. This can increase visibility and engagement, especially if the content aligns with your brand.

13. **Consistent Branding:**

- Maintain consistent branding across all content. This includes visual elements, tone of voice, and overall messaging. Consistency builds brand recognition.

14. **Ask Questions:**
- Pose questions to your audience. Encourage them to share their opinions, experiences, or advice. This fosters engagement and creates a dialogue.

15. **Live Videos and Q&A Sessions:**
- Incorporate live videos or Q&A sessions. Real-time interactions create a sense of immediacy and allow your audience to connect with your brand authentically.

Remember to monitor analytics to understand which types of content resonate most with your audience. Regularly analyze performance metrics and adjust your content strategy based on insights gained from audience engagement.

Types of Engaging Content

Creating diverse and engaging content is crucial for capturing the attention of your audience on social media. Here are various types of content that can foster engagement:

1. **Images and Graphics:**
- Visual content is highly shareable. Use high-quality images, infographics, and graphics to convey your message and capture attention.

2. **Videos:**
- Videos are powerful for storytelling. Create short-form videos, tutorials, behind-the-scenes clips, or even live videos to connect with your audience.

3. **Carousels:**
- Carousel posts allow you to share a series of images or slides in a single post. Use them to tell a sequential story, share tips, or showcase a product from different angles.

4. **Infographics:**

- Condense complex information into visually appealing infographics. This format is great for presenting statistics, processes, or step-by-step guides.

5. **Quotes and Text-based Content:**
- Share inspirational quotes, thought-provoking statements, or key messages. Well-designed text-based content can be visually striking and encourage sharing.

6. **Polls and Surveys:**
- Interactive content like polls and surveys invites audience participation. It's a fun way to gather feedback and involve your audience in decision-making.

7. **User-Generated Content (UGC):**
- Showcase content created by your followers or customers. Reposting UGC not only provides social proof but also encourages others to contribute.

8. **Behind-the-Scenes:**

- Take your audience behind the scenes of your business. Share glimpses of your workspace, production process, or introduce team members to humanize your brand.

9. **Tutorials and How-to Guides:**
- Educate your audience by creating tutorials or how-to guides. This type of content establishes your expertise and provides value to your followers.

10. **Interactive Stories:**
- Utilize features like Instagram Stories or Facebook Stories for interactive content. Include polls, quizzes, or ask questions to engage your audience.

11. **Contests and Giveaways:**
- Run contests or giveaways to encourage participation. This can boost brand awareness, increase followers, and generate excitement.

12. **Customer Testimonials:**

- Share customer testimonials or success stories. Authentic experiences from satisfied customers can build trust and credibility.

13. **Challenges and Trends:**
- Participate in popular challenges or trends. This can increase your visibility as you align your content with broader social media conversations.

14. **Live Q&A Sessions:**
- Conduct live Q&A sessions to connect directly with your audience. It allows for real-time interaction and builds a sense of community.

15. **Seasonal and Holiday Content:**
- Create content that aligns with seasons, holidays, or relevant events. This keeps your content timely and relatable.

Remember to analyze the performance of your content regularly. Understanding what types of content resonate most with your audience will help you refine your strategy for maximum engagement.

Visuals, Videos, and Infographics

Visuals, videos, and infographics are powerful content formats that can significantly enhance your social media strategy. Here's a closer look at each:

Visuals:

1. **High-Quality Images:**
- Share visually appealing and high-quality images that showcase your products, services, or brand personality. Clear, vibrant visuals catch the audience's attention.

2. **Branded Graphics:**
- Create branded graphics with your logo, color scheme, and key messages. Consistent branding enhances recognition and reinforces your brand identity.

3. **Quotes and Text Overlays:**
- Combine compelling quotes or key messages with striking visuals. This creates shareable content that communicates your brand values.

4. **Memes and Humorous Visuals:**
- When appropriate for your brand, use memes or humorous visuals. Humor can be highly shareable and helps create a more relatable brand image.

5. **Carousel Posts:**
- Use carousel posts to share a series of related images. This format allows you to tell a story or provide a step-by-step guide within a single post.

Videos:

1. **Short-form Videos:**
- Craft engaging short-form videos that are easy to consume on platforms like Instagram Reels or TikTok. Focus on capturing attention within the first few seconds.

2. **Behind-the-Scenes Footage:**
- Take your audience behind the scenes of your business. Showcasing your workspace, team, or production process humanizes your brand.

3. **Tutorials and How-to Videos:**
- Educate your audience with tutorials or how-to videos. Demonstrate product usage, share tips, or provide valuable insights related to your industry.

4. **Live Videos:**
- Utilize live videos for real-time interaction with your audience. Live Q&A sessions, product launches, or behind-the-scenes glimpses can foster engagement.

5. **Interviews and Collaborations:**
- Conduct interviews or collaborate with influencers, experts, or other brands. This not only provides valuable content but also broadens your reach through cross-promotion.

Infographics:

1. **Information Simplification:**
- Condense complex information into easy-to-understand infographics. Use visuals, icons, and minimal text to convey key points.

2. **Step-by-Step Guides:**
- Create infographics for step-by-step guides or processes. This format is excellent for conveying information in a structured and visually appealing manner.

3. **Statistical Information:**
- Present statistics or data in infographic form. Visualizing numbers makes the information more digestible and shareable.

4. **Comparisons and Contrasts:**
- Use infographics for comparisons, contrasts, or before-and-after scenarios. This format is effective for illustrating differences or showcasing improvements.

5. **Timeline Infographics:**

- Illustrate company milestones, product evolution, or historical events using timeline infographics. This format adds a storytelling element to your content.

Remember to tailor your content to each social media platform's specifications and audience behavior. A diverse mix of visuals, videos, and infographics contributes to a well-rounded and engaging social media presence. Analyze the performance of each type of content to refine your strategy over time.

User-Generated Content Strategies

Leveraging user-generated content (UGC) can be a powerful strategy to enhance your brand's authenticity, build community, and increase engagement on social media. Here are effective strategies to encourage and utilize user-generated content:

1. **Create a Branded Hashtag:**

- Develop a unique branded hashtag that users can use when posting content related to your brand. This not only encourages participation but also makes it easy to track and share UGC.

2. **Run Contests and Challenges:**
- Organize contests or challenges that prompt users to create and share content. This could involve photo contests, creative challenges, or sharing stories related to your products or services.

3. **Feature UGC on Your Platforms:**
- Showcase UGC on your official social media platforms. Repost photos, testimonials, or reviews from your customers, giving credit to the creators. This adds social proof and validates your brand.

4. **Encourage Reviews and Testimonials:**
- Request customers to share their experiences through reviews and testimonials. Highlight these on your website and social media channels. Positive reviews build trust and credibility.

5. **Host User Spotlight:**
- Feature a "User of the Month" or similar spotlight on your social media. Share the story of a customer or follower, including their UGC and what they love about your brand.

6. **Provide Incentives:**
- Offer incentives for users to create and share content. This could be discounts, exclusive access, or even the chance to be featured on your official channels. Incentives motivate participation.

7. **Create a Community:**
- Establish a community where users can connect, share experiences, and support each other. Platforms like Facebook Groups or dedicated community spaces foster engagement and UGC.

8. **Engage with UGC:**
- Respond to and engage with UGC actively. Thank users for their contributions, ask

follow-up questions, and create a positive and interactive environment.

9. **Collaborate with Influencers:**
- Partner with influencers in your industry who align with your brand. Encourage them to generate and share content related to your products or services. Influencers can significantly amplify UGC.

10. **Highlight Customer Stories:**
- Share customer success stories or transformation journeys. Visual and narrative content that showcases real people benefiting from your brand adds authenticity.

11. **Promote User-Generated Reviews:**
- Share screenshots or snippets of user-generated reviews across your social media. This not only provides valuable social proof but also encourages others to share their experiences.

12. **Utilize Instagram Stories Features:**

- Leverage Instagram's features like polls, quizzes, and question boxes to encourage interactive UGC. These features can prompt users to share their opinions, experiences, or feedback.

13. **Create UGC Campaigns:**
- Develop specific UGC campaigns with clear guidelines and themes. For example, ask users to share their favorite product uses or share photos wearing your merchandise.

14. **Show Appreciation:**
- Regularly express gratitude to your community for their support and contributions. Make your audience feel valued, and they'll be more likely to continue creating UGC.

Remember to establish clear guidelines for UGC to ensure that content aligns with your brand values. Monitor and moderate submissions to maintain a positive and brand-appropriate environment. By implementing these strategies, you can turn your audience into active contributors, creating a vibrant and engaged community around your brand.

Chapter 6
Community Building and Management

Building and managing a thriving community on social media involves strategic planning, active engagement, and consistent efforts to foster a positive and supportive environment. Here are key strategies for community building and management:

Community Building:

1. **Define Community Purpose:**
- Clearly define the purpose and goals of your community. Whether it's for product discussions, customer support, or industry networking, a clear purpose helps attract the right audience.

2. **Choose the Right Platform:**
- Select social media platforms that align with your community goals and where your target audience is most active. Different platforms cater to different types of communities.

3. **Create Engaging Content:**
- Develop content that sparks discussions, asks questions, and encourages participation. Regularly share valuable and relevant content to keep the community engaged.

4. **Establish Community Guidelines:**
- Set clear guidelines for community behavior. Clearly outline expectations regarding respect,

inclusivity, and the type of content allowed.
Enforce these guidelines consistently.

5. **Encourage Member Contributions:**
- Actively encourage community members to
contribute by asking questions, sharing
experiences, or posting relevant content.
Highlight and appreciate member contributions
regularly.

6. **Organize Events and Challenges:**
- Plan and host events, challenges, or themed
activities that align with your community's
interests. This adds variety and excitement,
fostering a sense of belonging.

7. **Incorporate Exclusive Content:**
- Offer exclusive content or benefits to
community members. This could include early
access to information, exclusive discounts, or
members-only content to incentivize
participation.

8. **Facilitate Networking:**

- Create opportunities for community members to connect with each other. This could involve networking events, introductions, or discussion threads where members can share their expertise.

Community Management:

1. **Moderation and Enforcement:**
- Regularly monitor community activity and enforce community guidelines. Address any inappropriate behavior promptly and consistently to maintain a positive atmosphere.

2. **Engage Actively:**
- Engage with community members regularly. Respond to comments, ask questions, and actively participate in discussions. Show that the community is a two-way communication channel.

3. **Recognize and Appreciate:**
- Acknowledge and appreciate active community members. Feature member

spotlights, host recognition events, or simply thank members for their contributions.

4. **Provide Timely Support:**
- If your community involves customer support, ensure that inquiries are addressed promptly. A timely and helpful response builds trust and loyalty among community members.

5. **Seek Feedback:**
- Actively seek feedback from the community. Ask for opinions on new features, content ideas, or ways to improve the community experience. This involvement creates a sense of ownership.

6. **Adapt and Evolve:**
- Be adaptable to the evolving needs and interests of your community. Regularly assess what is working well and what can be improved, and be open to making adjustments.

7. **Create Subgroups or Topics:**
- If your community is large, consider creating subgroups or topics to facilitate more focused

discussions. This helps members find information relevant to their interests.

8. **Promote User-Generated Content:**
- Encourage members to share their content and experiences within the community. This not only enriches the content but also empowers members to contribute actively.

9. **Handle Conflict Diplomatically:**
- In the case of conflicts or disagreements, address them diplomatically. Foster a culture of respectful communication and ensure that conflicts are resolved constructively.

Building and managing a community on social media is an ongoing process that requires dedication and genuine interest in fostering connections. By consistently providing value, engaging with members, and adapting to their needs, you can create a vibrant and supportive community around your brand.

Responding to Comments and Messages

Responding to comments and messages on social media is crucial for maintaining a positive relationship with your audience. Here are effective strategies for handling comments and messages:

Responding to Comments:

1. **Timely Responses:**
- Aim to respond to comments promptly. Timely responses show that you value your audience's engagement and are attentive to their interactions.

2. **Personalization:**
- Personalize your responses whenever possible. Address commenters by their names and tailor your responses to the specific content or question they raised.

3. **Express Gratitude:**
- Thank users for their comments, whether they're positive feedback, questions, or

constructive criticism. Expressing gratitude reinforces a positive relationship.

4. **Acknowledge and Validate:**
- Acknowledge the content of the comment and validate the user's perspective. Even if the comment is negative, acknowledging it shows that you are attentive and willing to address concerns.

5. **Encourage Further Engagement:**
- Encourage users to continue the conversation. Pose follow-up questions, invite them to share their experiences, or direct them to relevant content on your platform.

6. **Use Humor Appropriately:**
- If suitable for your brand voice and the context of the comment, injecting humor can be effective. However, be mindful of the tone and ensure it aligns with your brand image.

7. **Address Concerns Professionally:**

- Handle negative comments or concerns professionally and diplomatically. Avoid getting defensive and aim to resolve issues or direct users to appropriate support channels.

8. **Moderate Constructively:**
- If comments violate community guidelines, moderate them constructively. Remove inappropriate content while providing clear guidelines on community behavior.

Responding to Messages:

1. **Set Expectations:**
- Clearly communicate your response time expectations, especially if you cannot provide instant responses. This helps manage user expectations.

2. **Personalized Greetings:**
- Start your responses with personalized greetings, addressing users by their names. This adds a human touch to your interactions.

3. **Provide Helpful Information:**
- Offer valuable information in your responses.
If users have inquiries, strive to provide detailed
and helpful answers or direct them to the
appropriate resources.

4. **Direct to Support Channels:**
- If the message involves customer support or
complex issues, guide users to appropriate
support channels for more detailed assistance.
This ensures efficient problem resolution.

5. **Apologize for Delays:**
- If there are delays in responding,
acknowledge them and apologize. Transparency
about response times demonstrates
accountability.

6. **Maintain Professionalism:**
- Maintain a professional tone in your
messages. Even in casual interactions,
professionalism contributes to a positive brand
image.

7. **Use Emojis and Tone Indicators Appropriately:**
- If your brand allows for it, use emojis or tone indicators to convey friendliness and warmth. However, use them judiciously to maintain professionalism.

8. **Follow Up:**
- Follow up on previous interactions. If a user had a question or issue, check in to ensure they received the necessary assistance or information.

9. **Ask for Feedback:**
- Encourage users to provide feedback on their experience interacting with your brand through messages. This can help you identify areas for improvement.

By actively engaging with comments and messages, your brand demonstrates responsiveness and a commitment to customer satisfaction. Whether the interaction is positive or involves addressing concerns, each response contributes to building a strong and positive online presence.

Hosting Contests and Giveaways

Hosting contests and giveaways on social media can be a highly effective strategy for increasing engagement, expanding your reach, and creating excitement around your brand. Here's a guide on how to plan and execute successful contests and giveaways:

Planning:

1. **Define Objectives:**
- Clearly outline your goals for the contest or giveaway. Whether it's increasing brand awareness, growing your follower count, or promoting a new product, understanding your objectives is crucial.

2. **Choose the Right Platform:**
- Select the social media platform that aligns with your target audience and campaign goals.

Each platform has unique features for running contests, so choose accordingly.

3. **Establish Rules and Guidelines:**
- Clearly outline the rules and guidelines for participation. This includes eligibility criteria, entry methods, and any specific actions participants need to take (e.g., liking, sharing, tagging friends).

4. **Determine Prizes:**
- Decide on enticing prizes that align with your audience's interests. The prizes should be relevant to your brand and valuable enough to motivate participation.

5. **Set a Duration:**
- Determine the duration of the contest or giveaway. Whether it's a week-long promotion or a month-long campaign, ensure that the timeframe is sufficient for maximum participation.

6. **Promote Your Contest:**

- Create a promotional plan to generate buzz before the contest starts. Use teaser posts, countdowns, and engaging visuals to build anticipation.

Execution:

1. **Launch Creatively:**
- Launch your contest with an attention-grabbing post. Clearly communicate the entry requirements and highlight the prizes. Use visually appealing graphics or videos.

2. **Encourage User-Generated Content (UGC):**
- Incorporate UGC by asking participants to create and share content related to your brand. This could include photos, videos, or captions that align with the theme of the contest.

3. **Utilize Hashtags:**
- Create a unique and branded hashtag for your contest. Encourage participants to use the

hashtag when sharing their entries. This helps in
tracking and increases visibility.

4. **Engage with Participants:**
- Actively engage with participants by
responding to comments, liking their entries, and
sharing user-generated content on your official
page. This builds a sense of community and
excitement.

5. **Regular Updates:**
- Provide regular updates on the progress of
the contest. This could include highlighting
noteworthy entries, reminding participants of the
remaining time, or announcing milestones.

Winner Selection and Announcement:

1. **Fair and Transparent Selection:**
- Clearly outline the criteria for selecting
winners. Whether it's based on creativity,
adherence to rules, or random selection, ensure
that the process is fair and transparent.

2. **Announce Winners Publicly:**
- Once winners are selected, announce them publicly on your social media platforms. This could be done through a dedicated winner announcement post or a live video.

3. **Express Gratitude:**
- Express gratitude to all participants, whether they won or not. Acknowledge their efforts and encourage them to participate in future contests.

4. **Coordinate Prize Delivery:**
- Coordinate the delivery of prizes promptly. Clearly communicate the steps winners need to take to claim their prizes and provide any necessary contact information.

5. **Leverage User-Generated Content:**
- After the contest, continue leveraging UGC by showcasing entries or creating a highlights reel. This extends the reach and impact of your contest even after it concludes.

Post-Contest Evaluation:

1. **Analyze Results:**
- Analyze the results of your contest. Measure engagement metrics, follower growth, and any other key performance indicators relevant to your objectives.

2. **Seek Feedback:**
- Encourage participants to provide feedback on the contest experience. This can help you refine future contests and address any areas for improvement.

3. **Learn and Iterate:**
- Use the insights gained to inform your future contest strategies. Learning from each campaign allows you to iterate and optimize your approach for better results.

By carefully planning and executing contests and giveaways, you can turn them into powerful tools for brand promotion, audience engagement, and community building on social media.

Creating a Positive Community Culture

Creating a positive community culture on social media is essential for fostering engagement, building brand loyalty, and maintaining a supportive environment. Here are strategies to establish and nurture a positive community culture:

Establishing a Positive Culture:

1. **Define Core Values:**
- Clearly define the core values that your community upholds. These values should align with your brand identity and serve as the foundation for positive interactions.

2. **Set Community Guidelines:**
- Establish clear and comprehensive community guidelines. Clearly communicate expectations regarding behavior, language, and the type of content allowed. Ensure guidelines promote inclusivity and respect.

3. **Lead by Example:**
- Demonstrate the desired culture through your own interactions. Be respectful, positive, and responsive. Your community members will often take cues from your behavior.

4. **Encourage Diversity and Inclusion:**
- Foster a culture that celebrates diversity and inclusivity. Encourage members from different backgrounds, experiences, and perspectives to contribute, and ensure everyone feels valued.

5. **Promote Positivity:**
- Encourage positive interactions by highlighting and celebrating achievements, contributions, and uplifting content. Create an atmosphere where positivity is the norm.

Nurturing a Positive Community:

1. **Active Moderation:**
- Actively moderate the community to ensure adherence to guidelines. Promptly address any

inappropriate behavior or content. Consistent moderation reinforces the community's values.

2. **Provide Constructive Feedback:**
- When addressing issues, provide constructive feedback rather than focusing solely on punitive measures. Help members understand how their actions can contribute positively to the community.

3. **Highlight Member Contributions:**
- Regularly showcase and appreciate member contributions. This can include featuring member spotlights, sharing user-generated content, or acknowledging achievements.

4. **Encourage Collaboration:**
- Facilitate collaboration among community members. Encourage them to share insights, collaborate on projects, or support each other's endeavors. This strengthens bonds within the community.

5. **Celebrate Milestones:**

- Celebrate community milestones, whether it's reaching a certain number of members or achieving a collective goal. Recognition of shared achievements fosters a sense of belonging.

6. **Create a Supportive Environment:**
- Establish a supportive environment where members feel comfortable sharing their thoughts, questions, and concerns. Encourage mutual support and empathy.

7. **Facilitate Discussions:**
- Create discussion threads or forums that encourage meaningful conversations. Pose thought-provoking questions, share industry insights, or create spaces for members to share experiences.

8. **Address Issues Privately:**
- If conflicts arise, address them privately and diplomatically. Publicly airing grievances can escalate tensions and negatively impact the overall community atmosphere.

9. **Encourage Member-Led Initiatives:**
- Empower community members to take the lead on initiatives. Whether it's hosting events, starting discussions, or organizing collaborative projects, member-led activities contribute to a dynamic culture.

10. **Regular Communication:**
- Maintain open and transparent communication with the community. Keep members informed about updates, upcoming events, and any changes that may impact the community experience.

11. **Solicit Feedback:**
- Actively seek feedback from community members. Use surveys or discussion threads to gather input on their experiences and preferences. This involvement makes members feel heard and valued.

12. **Adapt and Iterate:**

- Be willing to adapt and iterate based on community feedback. As the community evolves, adjust strategies, guidelines, and activities to better align with members' needs and expectations.

By intentionally cultivating a positive community culture, you create an environment where members feel connected, engaged, and enthusiastic about contributing. Regularly assess the community dynamics, iterate based on feedback, and celebrate the positive culture you've collectively built.

Chapter 7
Leveraging Paid Advertising

Leveraging paid advertising on social media can significantly boost your brand's visibility, reach, and engagement. Here's a guide on how to effectively utilize paid advertising to meet your marketing goals:

Define Your Objectives:

1. **Clarify Goals:**
- Clearly define your advertising objectives. Whether it's increasing brand awareness, driving website traffic, generating leads, or boosting sales, having specific goals guides your campaign strategy.

2. **Identify Target Audience:**
- Clearly define your target audience. Understand their demographics, interests, and behaviors. This information is crucial for creating targeted and effective ad campaigns.

Choose the Right Platform:

1. **Platform Selection:**
- Select the social media platforms that align with your target audience. Different platforms cater to different demographics and interests.

2. **Consider Ad Formats:**
- Each platform offers various ad formats. Consider the type of content you want to promote and choose the ad format that best suits your campaign goals (e.g., image ads, video ads, carousel ads, etc.).

Develop Compelling Ad Creative:

1. **Eye-Catching Visuals:**
- Create visually appealing and eye-catching graphics or videos. High-quality visuals grab attention in the crowded social media feed.

2. **Compelling Copy:**

- Craft concise and compelling ad copy. Clearly communicate your message, value proposition, and call-to-action. Tailor the language to resonate with your target audience.

3. **Utilize Ad Extensions:**
- Take advantage of ad extensions to provide additional information or features. This can include site link extensions, callout extensions, and more, depending on the platform.

Targeting and Customization:

1. **Detailed Targeting:**
- Leverage detailed targeting options provided by the platform. Refine your audience based on demographics, interests, behaviors, and even past interactions with your brand.

2. **Custom Audiences:**
- Utilize custom audiences to target users who have already interacted with your brand, such as website visitors, email subscribers, or past customers. This can enhance retargeting efforts.

3. **Lookalike Audiences:**
- Create lookalike audiences to expand your reach to users who share characteristics with your existing audience. This helps in reaching new, potentially interested users.

Set Budgets and Bidding Strategies:

1. **Define Budgets:**
- Set clear budgets for your advertising campaigns. Allocate resources based on your overall marketing objectives and the expected return on investment (ROI).

2. **Bidding Strategy:**
- Choose an appropriate bidding strategy. Depending on your goals, you might opt for strategies like cost per click (CPC), cost per thousand impressions (CPM), or cost per acquisition (CPA).

Monitor and Optimize:

1. **Regular Monitoring:**
- Monitor the performance of your ads regularly. Track key metrics such as click-through rates, conversion rates, and return on ad spend (ROAS).

2. **A/B Testing:**
- Conduct A/B testing to optimize ad performance. Test different visuals, ad copies, and targeting options to identify what resonates best with your audience.

3. **Adjust Targeting Parameters:**
- Based on performance data, refine your targeting parameters. Narrow down or expand your audience based on what yields the best results.

4. **Optimize Landing Pages:**
- Ensure that the landing pages linked to your ads are optimized for conversion. A seamless transition from ad to landing page is crucial for a successful campaign.

5. **Ad Schedule Optimization:**
- Consider the timing of your ads. Optimize ad schedules to align with peak times when your target audience is most active.

Measure Results and Iteration:

1. **Analytics and Reporting:**
- Utilize platform analytics and reporting tools to measure the success of your campaigns. Evaluate which ads and strategies are delivering the best results.

2. **ROI Assessment:**
- Regularly assess the return on investment. Understand the cost-effectiveness of your campaigns and adjust your strategy accordingly.

3. **Iterate and Improve:**
- Based on the insights gathered, iterate and improve your future campaigns. Implement lessons learned from previous efforts to continually enhance performance.

Paid advertising on social media is a dynamic process that requires continuous optimization. By setting clear goals, understanding your audience, creating compelling content, and consistently monitoring and optimizing your campaigns, you can maximize the impact of your paid advertising efforts.

Targeted Ad Campaigns

Running targeted ad campaigns on social media allows you to reach specific audiences with tailored messages. Here's a step-by-step guide to creating effective targeted ad campaigns:

1. Define Your Target Audience:

1. **Demographic Targeting:**
- Identify key demographic factors such as age, gender, location, and income level. This helps you narrow down your audience based on basic characteristics.

2. **Behavioral Targeting:**

- Consider the behaviors and interests of your audience. This could include online activities, purchase behaviors, hobbies, or preferences. Use this information to refine your targeting.

3. **Psychographic Targeting:**
- Understand the psychographics of your audience, including values, attitudes, and lifestyle choices. This helps you create ads that resonate with the emotional aspects of your target audience.

4. **Custom Audiences:**
- Utilize custom audiences based on data you already have, such as website visitors, email subscribers, or past customers. This allows you to target users who have already shown interest in your brand.

5. **Lookalike Audiences:**
- Create lookalike audiences to expand your reach by targeting users who share characteristics with your existing customer base.

This is especially useful for reaching new potential customers.

2. Choose the Right Platform:

1. **Platform Alignment:**
- Select the social media platforms that align with your target audience. Different demographics and interests are prevalent on various platforms, so choose wisely.

2. **Ad Formats:**
- Consider the ad formats available on each platform. Some platforms offer carousel ads, video ads, story ads, and more. Choose the format that best suits your campaign objectives.

3. Craft Compelling Ad Creative:

1. **Tailor Messaging:**
- Customize your ad copy and visuals to resonate with the interests and preferences of your target audience. Speak directly to their needs and aspirations.

2. **Visual Appeal:**
- Create visually appealing graphics or videos that grab attention. Use high-quality images or videos that align with your brand and capture the essence of your message.

3. **Clear Call-to-Action (CTA):**
- Include a clear and compelling call-to-action. Whether it's encouraging a purchase, sign-up, or engagement, guide your audience on what action to take.

4. **Address Pain Points or Needs:**
- Identify the pain points or needs of your target audience and address them in your ad creative. Show how your product or service provides a solution or adds value.

4. Set Targeting Parameters:

1. **Geographic Targeting:**
- Refine your target audience based on geographic location. This can be as broad as

targeting a country or as specific as targeting users within a certain radius of your business.

2. **Interest and Behavior Targeting:**
- Use the platform's interest and behavior targeting options to reach users with specific interests or online behaviors that align with your product or service.

3. **Custom Audiences and Exclusions:**
- Refine your audience further by excluding specific groups or demographics. This ensures that your ads are reaching the most relevant users.

5. Define Budget and Schedule:

1. **Budget Allocation:**
- Set a budget for your ad campaign. Allocate your budget strategically based on the expected return on investment (ROI) for each segment of your target audience.

2. **Ad Schedule:**

- Consider the timing of your ads. Choose specific days and times to display your ads based on when your target audience is most active on the platform.

6. Monitor and Optimize:

1. **Regular Monitoring:**
- Monitor the performance of your targeted ad campaign regularly. Track key metrics such as click-through rates, conversion rates, and ad spend.

2. **A/B Testing:**
- Conduct A/B testing to optimize your ad elements. Test different headlines, images, and ad copies to identify what resonates best with your target audience.

3. **Adjust Targeting:**
- Based on performance data, refine your targeting parameters. This could involve narrowing down or expanding your audience based on what yields the best results.

4. **Optimize Landing Pages:**
- Ensure that the landing pages linked to your ads are optimized for the specific audience segment. A seamless transition from ad to landing page improves conversion rates.

7. Evaluate and Iterate:

1. **Analyze Results:**
- Utilize platform analytics and reporting tools to measure the success of your targeted ad campaign. Assess which audience segments and ad variations deliver the best results.

2. **ROI Assessment:**
- Regularly evaluate the return on investment. Understand the cost-effectiveness of your campaign and adjust your strategy accordingly.

3. **Iterate for Future Campaigns:**
- Use insights gathered from your targeted ad campaign to inform future campaigns. Apply

lessons learned to continuously refine and optimize your targeting strategy.

By meticulously defining your target audience, tailoring your ad creative, and optimizing based on performance data, you can create highly effective targeted ad campaigns that resonate with the right audience segments and drive meaningful results.

Budgeting and ROI Analysis

Budgeting and ROI analysis are critical components of a successful social media marketing strategy. Here's a guide to effectively manage your budget and analyze the return on investment (ROI):

Budgeting:

1. **Set Clear Objectives:**
- Clearly define your marketing objectives. Whether it's increasing brand awareness, driving

website traffic, or boosting sales, having specific goals will guide your budget allocation.

2. **Understand Platform Costs:**
- Familiarize yourself with the costs associated with advertising on different social media platforms. Each platform has its own pricing structure, and understanding these costs helps in budget planning.

3. **Define Overall Budget:**
- Set an overall budget for your social media marketing efforts. Consider both organic and paid strategies, including content creation, ad spend, and any additional expenses.

4. **Allocate Budget Strategically:**
- Allocate your budget strategically based on the priority of your marketing objectives. Consider allocating more budget to initiatives that align with your primary goals.

5. **Consider Ad Campaign Objectives:**

- If running paid ad campaigns, allocate budget based on campaign objectives. For example, brand awareness campaigns might have a different budget allocation compared to conversion-focused campaigns.

6. **Testing Budget:**
- Allocate a portion of your budget for testing. A/B testing different ad creatives, targeting options, or content strategies allows you to optimize your approach without overspending.

7. **Monitor and Adjust:**
- Regularly monitor the performance of your campaigns and adjust your budget as needed. If you find that certain strategies are delivering strong results, consider reallocating more budget to those areas.

ROI Analysis:

1. **Define Key Metrics:**
- Clearly define the key metrics you'll use to measure ROI. This could include metrics like

conversion rates, click-through rates, engagement metrics, and ultimately, revenue generated.

2. **Use Tracking and Analytics Tools:**
   - Implement tracking tools and analytics platforms to measure the performance of your social media efforts. Platforms like Google Analytics and social media analytics tools provide valuable insights.

3. **Attribution Modeling:**
- Understand the attribution model you'll use to attribute conversions or results to specific marketing channels. This helps in accurately assessing the impact of your social media efforts.

4. **Calculate Costs:**
- Calculate the total costs associated with your social media marketing efforts, including ad spend, content creation, and any other related expenses.

5. **Measure Conversions and Revenue:**
- Track conversions and revenue generated through your social media campaigns. Understand the direct impact on your business goals.

6. **Calculate ROI:**
- Use the following formula to calculate ROI: \[\text{ROI} = \left(\frac{\text{Net Profit}}{\text{Cost of Investment}} \right) \times 100 \] This formula considers the net profit generated as a result of your investment.

7. **Segment Results:**
- Segment your ROI analysis to understand the performance of individual campaigns or strategies. This provides insights into what is driving the most significant impact.

8. **Compare Against Benchmarks:**
- Compare your ROI against industry benchmarks or your own historical data. This context helps you understand how well your

social media efforts are performing relative to expectations.

9. **Iterate Based on Insights:**
- Use the insights gained from your ROI analysis to iterate and refine your social media strategy. Focus on optimizing the most effective channels and tactics.

10. **Consider Customer Lifetime Value (CLV):**
- If applicable to your business model, consider the customer lifetime value when assessing ROI. Understanding the long-term value of a customer provides a more comprehensive perspective.

11. **Regularly Review and Adjust:**
- ROI analysis is an ongoing process. Regularly review your results, make adjustments to your strategy, and refine your budget allocation based on what is delivering the best return.

By effectively budgeting and analyzing ROI, you can ensure that your social media efforts are not only aligned with your business goals but also providing a positive return on your investment. Regularly assessing and optimizing your strategy based on insights ensures that your social media marketing remains effective and efficient over time.

A/B Testing Strategies

A/B testing, also known as split testing, is a powerful method to optimize various elements of your social media campaigns. Here are key strategies for effective A/B testing on social media:

1. **Clearly Define Goals:**
- Start by clearly defining the goals of your A/B tests. Whether it's improving click-through rates, increasing conversions, or enhancing engagement, having specific objectives guides the testing process.

2. **Test One Element at a Time:**
- Focus on testing one element at a time to accurately identify what is impacting performance. Elements to test include headlines, ad copy, visuals, call-to-action buttons, and targeting parameters.

3. **A/B Testing on Ad Creatives:**
- **Visuals:** Test different images or videos to determine which resonates best with your audience.
- **Copy:** Experiment with variations in ad copy. Test different messaging tones, lengths, and formats.

4. **Headline Testing:**
- Assess the impact of different headlines on ad performance. Test variations in length, tone, and messaging to see which grabs the most attention.

5. **Call-to-Action (CTA) Testing:**

- Experiment with different CTAs to prompt different responses. Test variations in language, urgency, and placement of the CTA button.

6. **Audience Segmentation Testing:**
   - Test different audience segments to understand which groups respond best to your campaigns. This includes demographic, geographic, or behavioral segmentation.

7. **Ad Format Testing:**
   - If your platform supports multiple ad formats, test variations to see which format performs best. For example, compare the effectiveness of image ads versus carousel ads.

8. **Ad Placement Testing:**
- Experiment with different ad placements on the platform. Test whether your ads perform better in users' feeds, stories, or other placements.

9. **Testing Landing Pages:**

- If your social media campaign involves driving traffic to a landing page, A/B test different landing page variations. Evaluate the impact on conversion rates and user engagement.

10. **Testing Ad Scheduling:**
- Assess the performance of your ads at different times and days of the week. A/B test ad scheduling to identify optimal times for reaching your target audience.

11. **Ad Budget Testing:**
- Test different budget allocations to understand the impact on reach and engagement. This includes variations in daily or lifetime budgets.

12. **Use Statistical Significance:**
- Ensure that your results are statistically significant before drawing conclusions. This helps in avoiding premature decisions based on fluctuations in data.

13. **Segment Results:**

- Segment your results based on various
factors, such as demographics or device type.
This provides deeper insights into how different
audience segments respond to your variations.

14. **Iterate Based on Insights:**
- Use the insights gained from A/B testing to
iterate and refine your social media strategy.
Implement the most effective variations to
continuously optimize your campaigns.

15. **Document and Analyze Results:**
- Keep detailed records of your A/B tests and
their results. Regularly analyze the data to
identify patterns and trends that can inform
future strategies.

16. **Test Across Multiple Campaigns:**
- Extend your A/B testing strategies across
multiple campaigns to continually refine your
understanding of what works best for your
audience.

By systematically implementing A/B testing strategies, you can identify the most effective elements of your social media campaigns, optimize your approach, and continually improve performance over time. Regular testing is essential for staying responsive to changes in audience behavior and platform algorithms.

Chapter 8
Monitoring and Analytics

Effectively monitoring and analyzing your social media performance is crucial for refining your strategies, understanding audience behavior, and maximizing your impact. Here's a comprehensive guide on monitoring and analytics:

1. **Define Key Performance Indicators (KPIs):**
- Clearly define your KPIs based on your social media objectives. Common KPIs include engagement metrics (likes, shares, comments), reach, click-through rates, conversion rates, and follower growth.

2. **Use Social Media Analytics Tools:**
- Leverage built-in analytics tools provided by social media platforms (e.g., Facebook Insights, Twitter Analytics, Instagram Insights). These tools offer valuable data on performance metrics and audience demographics.

3. **Google Analytics Integration:**
- Integrate Google Analytics with your website to track social media-driven traffic, conversions, and user behavior on your site. This provides a

comprehensive view of how social media impacts your website.

4. **Set Up UTM Parameters:**
- Use UTM parameters in your social media links to track campaign performance accurately in Google Analytics. This allows you to attribute specific actions on your website to social media campaigns.

5. **Regularly Monitor Engagement:**
- Monitor engagement metrics such as likes, shares, comments, and click-through rates. Identify content that resonates with your audience and adjust your content strategy accordingly.

6. **Track Follower Growth:**
- Keep track of your follower growth over time. Analyze periods of significant growth or decline to understand the impact of your content and campaigns.

7. **Audience Demographics:**

- Understand your audience demographics through platform insights. Analyze data on age, gender, location, and interests to tailor your content to your audience's preferences.

8. **Content Performance Analysis:**
- Analyze the performance of individual pieces of content. Identify high-performing posts and assess the common elements contributing to their success.

9. **Conversion Tracking:**
- Implement conversion tracking to measure the impact of social media on specific business goals, such as sign-ups, purchases, or lead generation.

10. **Sentiment Analysis:**
- Use sentiment analysis tools to gauge the sentiment of mentions and comments related to your brand. This helps in understanding how your audience perceives your brand on social media.

11. **Competitor Analysis:**
- Monitor and analyze the social media activities of your competitors. Gain insights into their strategies, content performance, and audience engagement to inform your own approach.

12. **Social Listening:**
- Engage in social listening to monitor mentions of your brand or relevant industry keywords. This helps you stay informed about conversations related to your brand and industry.

13. **Benchmark Against Goals:**
- Regularly benchmark your performance against the goals you've set. Assess whether you're meeting, exceeding, or falling short of your social media objectives.

14. **Identify Trends:**
- Identify trends in your social media data. Look for patterns in content performance, audience engagement, and follower behavior to capitalize on emerging opportunities.

15. **Ad Campaign Performance:**
- Analyze the performance of your paid advertising campaigns. Evaluate key metrics such as click-through rates, conversion rates, and return on ad spend (ROAS).

16. **Reporting and Documentation:**
- Create regular reports summarizing your social media analytics. Document insights, trends, and recommendations for future strategies. This documentation is valuable for tracking progress over time.

17. **Iterate Based on Insights:**
- Use the insights gained from monitoring and analytics to iterate and refine your social media strategy. Implement changes based on what is proven to be effective.

18. **Stay Informed About Platform Changes:**
- Stay updated on changes to social media algorithms and features. Platforms often

introduce updates that can impact your visibility and engagement.

19. **Experiment with New Strategies:**
- Use your analytics to identify areas for improvement and experimentation. Test new content formats, posting schedules, or engagement tactics based on your data-driven insights.

By consistently monitoring and analyzing your social media performance, you can make informed decisions, optimize your strategies, and ensure that your efforts align with your overall business objectives. Regular evaluation and adaptation are key to a successful and evolving social media presence.

Key Metrics for Social Media Success

Key metrics for social media success vary depending on your specific goals and objectives. However, here are some commonly used metrics that can help you assess the effectiveness of your social media efforts:

1. **Engagement Metrics:**
- **Likes, Shares, Comments:** Measure the interactions users have with your content. Higher engagement indicates that your audience finds your content valuable and engaging.

2. **Reach and Impressions:**
- **Reach:** The number of unique users who see your content.
- **Impressions:** The total number of times your content is displayed, including multiple views by the same user. Monitoring reach and impressions helps you understand the extent of your content's visibility.

3. **Follower Growth:**
- Track the growth of your follower base over time. A steady increase indicates a growing and engaged audience.

4. **Click-Through Rate (CTR):**

- Measure the percentage of people who clicked on your content after seeing it. CTR is crucial for assessing the effectiveness of your call-to-action and the relevance of your content.

5. **Conversion Rate:**
- For campaigns with specific goals (e.g., sign-ups, purchases), measure the percentage of users who completed the desired action. Conversion rate reflects the effectiveness of your social media funnel.

6. **Referral Traffic:**
- Monitor the amount of traffic directed to your website from social media. This helps you understand the impact of your social media efforts on website visits.

7. **Brand Mentions:**
- Keep track of mentions of your brand across social media platforms. Positive mentions contribute to brand reputation, while negative mentions may require attention and response.

8. **Audience Demographics:**
- Understand the demographics of your social media audience. Platforms often provide insights into age, gender, location, and interests. Tailor your content to match the preferences of your audience.

9. **Social Listening Sentiment:**
- Gauge the sentiment of mentions related to your brand or industry through social listening tools. Positive sentiment is an indicator of a positive brand perception.

10. **Time Spent on Page:**
- If your social media campaigns direct users to specific landing pages, track the time users spend on those pages. This metric provides insights into the level of engagement with your content.

11. **Cost per Click (CPC) or Cost per Conversion:**
- For paid advertising campaigns, measure the cost associated with each click or conversion.

This helps assess the cost-effectiveness of your paid efforts.

12. **Video Metrics:**
- **Views:** Measure the number of views for your videos.
- **Watch Time:** Track how much time users spend watching your videos.
- **Engagement:** Assess likes, comments, and shares specific to your video content.

13. **Customer Lifetime Value (CLV):**
- If applicable, track the lifetime value of customers acquired through social media. This metric helps in understanding the long-term impact of your social media efforts on revenue.

14. **Social Shares:**
- Track the number of times your content is shared on social media platforms. Shared content extends your reach beyond your immediate audience.

15. **Response Time:**

- Measure the time it takes for your brand to respond to customer inquiries or comments. A quick response time is crucial for maintaining positive customer relationships.

16. **Sentiment Analysis:**
- Use sentiment analysis tools to gauge the overall sentiment of discussions related to your brand on social media. This provides insights into the general perception of your brand.

17. **Competitive Metrics:**
- Monitor metrics related to your competitors, such as their engagement rates, follower growth, and content performance. This helps you benchmark your performance against industry peers.

18. **Return on Investment (ROI):**
- Assess the financial impact of your social media efforts. Compare the costs of your campaigns to the revenue generated or other tangible business outcomes.

19. **Customer Feedback and Reviews:**
- Track customer feedback and reviews received through social media. Positive reviews contribute to brand credibility, while negative feedback may require prompt attention.

20. **Influencer Metrics:**
- If collaborating with influencers, monitor metrics such as reach, engagement, and the impact of influencer partnerships on your brand.

Selecting the most relevant metrics for your specific goals and regularly analyzing them will help you make data-driven decisions, refine your social media strategies, and demonstrate the impact of your efforts on overall business objectives.

Analyzing Data for Continuous Improvement

Analyzing data for continuous improvement is a fundamental aspect of refining your social media strategies. Here's a step-by-step guide to effectively analyze data and drive continuous improvement:

1. **Set Clear Objectives:**
- Start with clearly defined social media objectives. Ensure that your goals are specific, measurable, achievable, relevant, and time-bound (SMART).

2. **Define Key Metrics:**
- Identify key performance indicators (KPIs) that align with your objectives. These metrics serve as benchmarks for assessing the success of your social media efforts.

3. **Regular Monitoring:**
- Establish a routine for regularly monitoring your social media metrics. This may involve daily, weekly, or monthly check-ins, depending on the nature of your campaigns.

4. **Compare Against Benchmarks:**
- Benchmark your current performance against historical data or industry benchmarks. This

comparison provides context for understanding whether your metrics are improving or declining.

5. **Identify Trends:**
- Look for trends in your data over time. Identify patterns related to engagement spikes, follower growth, or changes in audience behavior. Trends can inform adjustments to your strategy.

6. **Segment Results:**
- Segment your data based on various factors such as demographics, content types, or campaign variations. This segmentation provides more granular insights into what works best.

7. **Understand Audience Insights:**
- Utilize audience insights available on social media platforms. Understand the demographics, interests, and behaviors of your audience to tailor your content accordingly.

8. **A/B Testing Analysis:**

- Analyze the results of A/B testing initiatives. Identify variations that perform better and incorporate those insights into your ongoing strategy.

9. **Evaluate Content Performance:**
- Assess the performance of individual pieces of content. Identify high-performing content and understand the characteristics that contribute to its success.

10. **Conversion Path Analysis:**
- If applicable, analyze the user journey from social media to conversions on your website. Identify touchpoints where users drop off or convert to optimize the conversion path.

11. **Feedback Analysis:**
- Review user comments, mentions, and feedback on social media. Use this qualitative data to understand audience sentiment, preferences, and areas for improvement.

12. **Assess Paid Campaigns:**

- Evaluate the performance of paid advertising campaigns. Measure key metrics such as click-through rates, conversion rates, and return on ad spend (ROAS).

13. **Adapt Based on Seasonality:**
- Consider seasonal variations in your data. Adjust your content strategy or campaigns to align with trends and events that may impact user behavior.

14. **Identify Pain Points:**
- Identify any pain points or challenges revealed by the data. Whether it's a decline in engagement or an issue with a specific campaign, addressing these challenges is essential for improvement.

15. **ROI Assessment:**
- Regularly assess the return on investment (ROI) of your social media efforts. Understand the financial impact of your campaigns and adjust strategies to maximize ROI.

16. **Customer Journey Mapping:**
- Map the customer journey from social media awareness to conversion. Identify touchpoints where improvements can be made to enhance the overall user experience.

17. **Iterate Based on Insights:**
- Use the insights gathered to iterate and refine your social media strategy. Implement changes based on what is proven to be effective in achieving your objectives.

18. **Document Learnings:**
- Document key learnings and insights from your data analysis. This documentation serves as a valuable resource for making informed decisions in the future.

19. **Share Insights Across Teams:**
- Collaborate with other teams, such as marketing, sales, and customer support, to share insights and align strategies. Cross-functional collaboration enhances the impact of your efforts.

20. **Stay Informed About Platform Changes:**
- Stay updated on changes to social media algorithms, features, and policies. Adapt your strategy to leverage new opportunities or mitigate challenges introduced by platform updates.

By consistently analyzing data and incorporating insights into your strategy, you create a cycle of continuous improvement. This iterative approach ensures that your social media efforts remain dynamic, responsive to changes, and aligned with your overarching business objectives.

Tools for Monitoring and Reporting

There are several tools available to assist you in monitoring and reporting on your social media performance. Here's a list of popular tools that can help you gather insights, track metrics, and create comprehensive reports:

Social Media Analytics Tools:

1. **Hootsuite:**
- Hootsuite allows you to manage and schedule posts across multiple social media platforms. It also provides analytics to track engagement, follower growth, and more.

2. **Buffer:**
- Buffer simplifies social media scheduling and provides analytics on post performance, including reach, clicks, and engagement.

3. **Sprout Social:**
- Sprout Social offers a comprehensive suite of social media management tools, including analytics, social listening, and reporting features.

4. **Later:**
- Later is primarily a visual content scheduler for Instagram, but it also offers analytics to track engagement and audience growth.

Platform-Specific Analytics:

5. **Facebook Insights:**
- Facebook's native analytics tool provides in-depth insights into page performance, audience demographics, and engagement metrics.

6. **Twitter Analytics:**
- Twitter's native analytics platform offers data on tweet performance, audience demographics, and engagement.

7. **Instagram Insights:**
- Instagram provides insights within the app, offering data on post reach, interactions, and audience demographics.

8. **LinkedIn Analytics:**
- LinkedIn's analytics tool provides data on post engagement, follower demographics, and page views.

Google Analytics:

9. **Google Analytics:**
- While not a social media-specific tool, Google Analytics helps track website traffic originating from social media, providing insights into user behavior and conversions.

Social Listening Tools:

10. **Brandwatch:**
- Brandwatch is a social listening tool that helps you monitor brand mentions, track sentiment, and understand audience perceptions.

11. **Talkwalker:**
- Talkwalker offers social media analytics and listening capabilities, helping you track brand mentions and analyze sentiment across various platforms.

Reporting Tools:

12. **Google Data Studio:**
- Google Data Studio allows you to create customizable and interactive reports by pulling

data from various sources, including social media platforms and Google Analytics.

13. **Sprout Social Reports:**
- Sprout Social provides detailed reporting features, allowing you to create visual and comprehensive reports on social media performance.

14. **Buffer Analyze:**
- Buffer's Analyze feature offers in-depth analytics and reporting capabilities, enabling you to create detailed reports on social media metrics.

15. **Hootsuite Analytics:**
- Hootsuite's analytics tool provides detailed reports on key social media metrics, including engagement, follower growth, and post performance.

Influencer Marketing Tools:

16. **Traackr:**

- Traackr is an influencer marketing platform that helps you identify, manage, and measure the impact of influencers on your social media campaigns.

17. **AspireIQ:**
- AspireIQ is an influencer marketing platform that assists in discovering influencers, managing campaigns, and analyzing performance metrics.

These tools offer a range of features, from scheduling and posting content to in-depth analytics and social listening. Depending on your specific needs and the platforms you use, you can choose a combination of tools to effectively monitor, analyze, and report on your social media performance.

Chapter 9

Staying Updated on Trends

Staying updated on trends is crucial for maintaining a relevant and effective social media strategy. Here are some strategies to stay informed about the latest trends in the dynamic world of social media:

1. **Follow Industry News and Blogs:**
- Regularly read industry-specific blogs, news websites, and publications dedicated to social media marketing. This includes platforms like Social Media Today, Social Media Examiner, and HubSpot's Marketing Blog.

2. **Subscribe to Newsletters:**
- Subscribe to newsletters from social media platforms, marketing agencies, and influencers. Newsletters often provide curated content and insights on emerging trends and best practices.

3. **Attend Webinars and Virtual Events:**

- Participate in webinars, virtual conferences, and online events related to social media marketing. These events often feature industry experts sharing insights on the latest trends and strategies.

4. **Join Online Communities:**
- Engage in online communities and forums dedicated to social media marketing. Platforms like LinkedIn Groups, Reddit, or specialized forums offer discussions on current trends and challenges.

5. **Follow Influencers and Thought Leaders:**
- Follow influencers, thought leaders, and experts in the field of social media marketing on platforms like Twitter, LinkedIn, and Instagram. Their content often highlights trends and provides valuable insights.

6. **Utilize Social Media Platforms:**
- Actively use social media platforms to explore trending topics, hashtags, and

discussions within your industry. Follow relevant accounts to stay updated on the latest news and trends.

7. **Explore Trending Hashtags:**
- Monitor trending hashtags on platforms like Twitter and Instagram. Hashtags often reflect current events, discussions, and trends within the social media landscape.

8. **Set Up Google Alerts:**
- Set up Google Alerts for keywords related to social media marketing. Receive notifications when new content, news articles, or blog posts are published on topics of interest.

9. **Engage in Podcasts:**
- Listen to podcasts dedicated to social media marketing. Podcasts are an excellent medium for staying informed while multitasking or during commutes.

10. **Experiment with New Features:**

- Stay updated on new features and updates rolled out by social media platforms. Experiment with these features to understand how they can be incorporated into your strategy.

11. **Monitor Competitor Activity:**
- Keep an eye on the social media activities of your competitors. Analyzing their strategies can provide insights into emerging trends and innovative approaches.

12. **Read Research Reports:**
- Explore research reports and studies related to social media marketing. Reports from organizations like Pew Research Center and social media platforms themselves often include valuable data and trends.

13. **Network with Peers:**
- Network with fellow professionals in the field. Attend industry events, join networking groups, and participate in discussions to gain insights from peers.

14. **Continuously Learn and Certify:**
- Invest in continuous learning through online courses, certifications, and workshops. Platforms like HubSpot Academy, LinkedIn Learning, and Google Digital Garage offer courses on social media marketing.

15. **Stay Informed About Platform Updates:**
- Follow official blogs and updates from social media platforms to be aware of changes to algorithms, policies, and new features.

16. **Experiment with Emerging Platforms:**
- Keep an eye on emerging social media platforms and experiment with them to understand their potential. Early adoption can give you a competitive advantage.

17. **Read Books on Social Media Marketing:**
- Explore books on social media marketing written by industry experts. Books provide

in-depth insights into strategies, trends, and case studies.

18. **Attend Physical Conferences and Workshops:**
- Attend physical conferences and workshops when possible. Face-to-face interactions with industry experts and professionals can provide valuable insights.

By incorporating these strategies into your routine, you can create a proactive approach to staying updated on trends in social media marketing. Regularly dedicating time to learning and exploration ensures that your strategies remain innovative and aligned with the evolving landscape of social media.

Emerging Social Media Trends

As of my last knowledge update in January 2022, several social media trends were gaining traction. Keep in mind that trends evolve, and new ones may have emerged since then. Here are some emerging social media trends that were notable at that time:

1. **Short-Form Video Content:**
- The rise of short-form video content on platforms like TikTok and Instagram Reels was a significant trend. Brands were exploring creative ways to engage audiences through quick, visually appealing videos.

2. **Live Streaming and Virtual Events:**
- Live streaming gained popularity for real-time engagement. Businesses and influencers were leveraging live sessions for Q&A, product launches, and virtual events, providing an authentic connection with their audience.

3. **Ephemeral Content:**
- Ephemeral content, which disappears after a short period, was on the rise. Stories on platforms like Instagram and Snapchat allowed for casual, in-the-moment content sharing.

4. **Social Commerce Integration:**
- Social media platforms were increasingly integrating e-commerce features. Instagram Shopping, Facebook Shops, and other tools enabled businesses to sell products directly through their social media profiles.

5. **Augmented Reality (AR) Filters:**
- AR filters on platforms like Instagram and Snapchat were becoming popular for enhancing user engagement. Brands were using AR to create interactive and entertaining content.

6. **Inclusivity and Diversity:**
- There was a growing emphasis on inclusivity and diversity in content. Brands were focusing on representing diverse voices and perspectives to connect with a broader audience.

7. **Employee Advocacy:**
- Companies were encouraging employee advocacy on social media. Leveraging employees as brand advocates helped in

humanizing the brand and reaching new audiences.

8. **Niche Communities and Micro-Influencers:**
- Niche communities and micro-influencers were gaining attention for their ability to create highly targeted and authentic content. Brands were collaborating with influencers with smaller, engaged audiences.

9. **Audio-First Platforms:**
- The rise of audio-first platforms like Clubhouse and the introduction of audio features on other platforms signaled a shift toward more immersive audio content and conversations.

10. **Sustainability and Social Responsibility:**
- Socially responsible and sustainable practices were becoming integral to brand messaging. Consumers were showing a preference for brands that demonstrated a commitment to social and environmental causes.

11. **Personalized and Interactive Content:**
- Personalization in content and interactive elements, such as polls, quizzes, and interactive posts, were being used to enhance user engagement and gather valuable insights.

12. **Messaging Apps for Business:**
- Businesses were increasingly using messaging apps for customer communication and support. Platforms like WhatsApp and Facebook Messenger were becoming essential for brand-consumer interactions.

13. **Algorithm Changes and Organic Reach:**
- Changes in social media algorithms were impacting organic reach. Brands were focusing on creating highly engaging and shareable content to navigate algorithmic changes.

14. **Visual Search:**

- Visual search capabilities were gaining prominence, allowing users to search and shop for products directly through images. Pinterest and Google Lens were at the forefront of this trend.

15. **Gamification:**
- Gamification elements, such as contests, challenges, and interactive games, were being used to boost engagement and create a more interactive user experience.

To stay current with the latest social media trends, consider checking recent industry reports, following updates from major social media platforms, and keeping an eye on reputable marketing publications. Social media trends evolve rapidly, so staying informed allows you to adapt and incorporate relevant strategies into your social media marketing efforts.

Adaptive Strategies for Changing Platforms

Adapting to changing social media platforms is crucial for maintaining an effective online presence. Here are adaptive strategies to navigate shifts in social media platforms:

1. **Stay Informed About Platform Changes:**
- Regularly check for updates, feature changes, and algorithm adjustments on social media platforms. Follow official blogs, newsletters, and announcements to stay informed.

2. **Diversify Platform Presence:**
- Diversify your social media presence across multiple platforms. This provides flexibility and reduces dependence on any single platform.

3. **Monitor User Behavior:**
- Analyze user behavior and engagement patterns on different platforms. Understand how your audience interacts with content and adapt your strategy accordingly.

4. **Experiment with New Features:**

- Actively explore and experiment with new features introduced by platforms. Early adoption can provide a competitive advantage and enhance visibility.

5. **Responsive Content Creation:**
- Create content that aligns with the format and preferences of each platform. Tailor your content to match the audience expectations on specific platforms.

6. **Adjust Posting Schedule:**
- Monitor the times when your audience is most active on each platform. Adjust your posting schedule to maximize visibility during peak engagement periods.

7. **Utilize Cross-Promotion:**
- Cross-promote content across different platforms to encourage followers to connect with your brand on multiple channels. This reinforces your overall online presence.

8. **Optimize for Mobile:**

- Given the prevalence of mobile usage, ensure that your content is optimized for mobile viewing and interaction. Consider the mobile experience when designing visuals and layouts.

9. **Engage with New Trends:**
   - Stay attuned to emerging trends and challenges on each platform. Engage with popular hashtags, challenges, and discussions to remain relevant and visible.

10. **Collaborate with Influencers:**
   - Collaborate with influencers who are active on various platforms. Influencers can help amplify your message and reach diverse audiences.

11. **Adapt to Algorithm Changes:**
   - Understand how algorithm changes on platforms impact content visibility. Adapt your content strategy to align with algorithmic preferences and maximize organic reach.

12. **Listen to Audience Feedback:**

- Actively listen to audience feedback on each platform. Use comments, messages, and insights to understand user preferences and make adjustments.

13. **Invest in Paid Advertising:**
- Consider allocating budget for paid advertising on platforms. Paid campaigns can help maintain visibility, especially during times of algorithmic shifts.

14. **Evaluate Platform Effectiveness:**
- Regularly assess the effectiveness of each platform in achieving your goals. Allocate resources based on the platforms that yield the best results for your brand.

15. **Build an Email List:**
- As a supplementary strategy, build an email list to establish a direct line of communication with your audience. Email marketing can provide stability amid platform changes.

16. **Crisis Preparedness:**

- Develop crisis management plans in case of unexpected changes or challenges on a platform. Be prepared to adapt quickly and communicate effectively with your audience.

17. **Data-Driven Decision-Making:**
- Utilize analytics and insights to inform your decisions. Regularly analyze data to understand performance and make informed adjustments to your strategy.

18. **Educate Team Members:**
- Ensure that your team members are well-informed about changes on social media platforms. Invest in ongoing education to enhance their adaptability.

19. **Stay Agile and Flexible:**
- Embrace an agile and flexible mindset. Social media is dynamic, and the ability to adapt quickly is a key factor in long-term success.

Adapting to changing social media platforms requires a proactive and strategic approach. By staying informed, experimenting with new features, and actively engaging with your audience, you can navigate shifts in the social media landscape and maintain a resilient online presence.

Case Studies of Successful Campaigns

Certainly! Here are brief summaries of three successful social media campaigns:

1. **ALS Ice Bucket Challenge (2014):**
   - **Objective:** Raise awareness and funds for amyotrophic lateral sclerosis (ALS) research.
   - **Strategy:** Participants were challenged to pour a bucket of ice water over their heads, share the video on social media, and nominate others to do the same.
   - **Results:** The campaign went viral globally, with millions of participants, including celebrities. It raised over $115 million for the ALS Association and significantly increased awareness about the disease.

2. **Dove Real Beauty Campaign (2004 - Present):**
- **Objective:** Challenge beauty stereotypes and promote real beauty.
- **Strategy:** The campaign features real women in their natural beauty, embracing diversity and challenging traditional beauty standards. It includes videos, advertisements, and social media content.
- **Results:** Dove's Real Beauty Campaign garnered widespread praise, increased brand loyalty, and sparked important conversations about beauty standards. The campaign has evolved over the years, maintaining its impact.

3. **#ShareACoke (2014):**
- **Objective:** Increase Coca-Cola sales and engage with consumers.
- **Strategy:** Coca-Cola replaced its logo with popular names and phrases on its bottles and cans, encouraging people to share a Coke with friends and family. Social media played a central role in sharing personalized Coke bottles.

- **Results:** The campaign generated a significant social media buzz. Over 150 million personalized Coke bottles were distributed, and Coca-Cola experienced a 2% increase in U.S. sales after a decade of decline.

These case studies highlight the power of creativity, engagement, and a strong message in social media campaigns. Successful campaigns often tap into emotions, leverage user-generated content, and foster a sense of community, contributing to both brand awareness and tangible results.

Chapter 10
Crisis Management

Crisis management on social media is crucial for protecting a brand's reputation and maintaining customer trust. Here's a guide to effective crisis management on social media:

1. **Develop a Crisis Management Plan:**
   - **Preparation is Key:** Develop a comprehensive crisis management plan that outlines potential scenarios, response protocols, and the roles of team members.

2. **Monitor Social Media Channels:**
   - **Real-Time Monitoring:** Regularly monitor social media channels for mentions of your brand. Use social listening tools to track conversations and identify potential issues before they escalate.

3. **Identify the Type of Crisis:**

- **Categorize the Crisis:** Understand the nature of the crisis—whether it's a product issue, customer service problem, or a public relations challenge. Tailor your response accordingly.

4. **Quick Response Time:**
- **Timely Response:** Respond swiftly to emerging crises. Acknowledge the issue and reassure your audience that you are addressing it. Delayed responses can escalate the situation.

5. **Designate a Spokesperson:**
- **Centralized Communication:** Designate a single spokesperson to communicate with the public. This ensures a consistent and controlled flow of information.

6. **Be Transparent and Honest:**
- **Open Communication:** Be transparent about the situation. Provide accurate information and avoid misleading or vague statements. Honesty builds trust.

7. **Apologize Sincerely:**

- **Sincere Apology:** If your brand is at fault, issue a sincere apology. Acknowledge the impact on customers and outline steps being taken to resolve the issue.

8. **Move the Conversation Offline:**
- **Transition to Private Channels:** When appropriate, encourage individuals to move the conversation to private channels like direct messages or customer service hotlines to address issues more personally.

9. **Educate and Update:**
- **Inform and Educate:** Provide regular updates on the situation and the actions being taken to resolve it. Educate your audience about preventive measures or solutions.

10. **Activate Pre-Approved Messaging:**
- **Prepared Statements:** Have pre-approved messaging ready for common crisis scenarios. This ensures consistency and reduces the risk of miscommunication.

11. **Engage Positively:**
- **Positivity Amid Crisis:** Respond to negative comments with empathy and a positive tone. Avoid confrontations and focus on resolving issues constructively.

12. **Use Social Media Platforms Effectively:**
- **Leverage Features:** Use platform-specific features to address issues. For example, Twitter threads, Instagram Stories, or Facebook updates can provide ongoing information.

13. **Monitor Sentiment:**
- **Sentiment Analysis:** Continuously analyze sentiment to gauge how the crisis is impacting brand perception. Adjust your strategy based on sentiment trends.

14. **Learn and Adapt:**
- **Post-Crisis Analysis:** After the crisis is resolved, conduct a thorough analysis. Identify

lessons learned, areas for improvement, and update your crisis management plan accordingly.

15. **Post-Crisis Communication:**
- **Rebuilding Trust:** Communicate your commitment to preventing similar issues in the future. Highlight corrective actions taken and emphasize the lessons learned.

16. **Train Your Team:**
- **Continuous Training:** Regularly train your social media and customer service teams on crisis management procedures. Ensure they are equipped to handle different scenarios.

17. **Legal and Compliance Considerations:**
- **Legal Guidance:** In certain crises, legal considerations may be relevant. Consult with legal experts to ensure that your responses comply with regulations.

18. **Audit Your Social Media Presence:**

- **Regular Audits:** Periodically audit your social media presence for potential vulnerabilities. Proactively address any issues to minimize the risk of crises.

19. **Stay Calm and Composed:**
- **Leadership Presence:** Maintain a calm and composed leadership presence during a crisis. Project confidence and control to reassure both your team and the public.

20. **Post-Crisis Evaluation:**
- **Performance Review:** After the crisis is fully addressed, conduct a comprehensive review. Evaluate the effectiveness of your response, communication, and overall crisis management strategy.

Proactive and strategic crisis management on social media involves a combination of preparation, transparency, and effective communication. By implementing these strategies, brands can navigate crises with resilience and protect their online reputation.

Preparing for Potential Crises

Preparation for potential crises is essential for effectively managing and mitigating the impact of unforeseen challenges. Here's a guide on how to prepare for potential crises on social media:

1. **Conduct a Risk Assessment:**
- Identify Potential Risks: Assess potential risks and vulnerabilities specific to your industry, brand, and social media presence. Consider issues related to products, customer service, public relations, and external factors.

2. **Develop a Crisis Management Plan:**
- Create a Detailed Plan: Develop a comprehensive crisis management plan that outlines specific procedures, responsibilities, and communication protocols. Include potential crisis scenarios, key contacts, and pre-approved messaging.

3. **Establish a Crisis Management Team:**

- Designate Roles: Form a dedicated crisis management team with clearly defined roles and responsibilities. This team should include representatives from social media, public relations, customer service, legal, and senior management.

4. **Implement Social Listening:**
- Monitor Conversations: Utilize social listening tools to monitor conversations about your brand, industry, and relevant keywords. Regularly track sentiment, identify emerging issues, and stay informed about potential crises.

5. **Set up Alerts and Notifications:**
- Automated Alerts: Implement automated alerts for specific keywords, mentions, or sudden changes in sentiment. This allows for quick identification and response to potential crises.

6. **Develop Pre-Approved Messaging:**
- Prepared Statements: Create pre-approved messaging for common crisis scenarios. Having pre-drafted statements ensures a timely and

consistent response during the initial stages of a crisis.

7. **Conduct Crisis Simulations:**
- Scenario-Based Exercises: Regularly conduct crisis simulations and scenario-based exercises with your crisis management team. This helps refine processes, test response times, and identify areas for improvement.

8. **Establish Communication Protocols:**
- Communication Channels: Define communication channels and protocols for internal and external communication during a crisis. Ensure that all team members are aware of the preferred channels for information sharing.

9. **Provide Training for Team Members:**
- Continuous Training: Train your social media, customer service, and crisis management teams on crisis procedures. Ensure they understand their roles and responsibilities, as

well as how to use communication tools effectively.

10. **Create a Crisis Communication Hub:**
- Centralized Information: Establish a centralized crisis communication hub where your team can access relevant information, updates, and messaging templates. This ensures that everyone is working from a consistent source of information.

11. **Establish Media Contacts:**
- Media Relations: Identify and establish relationships with key media contacts. In the event of a crisis, having designated media spokespeople can help manage external communications effectively.

12. **Legal and Compliance Review:**
- Legal Guidance: Consult with legal experts to ensure that your crisis management plan and responses comply with relevant regulations.

Address potential legal considerations in advance.

13. **Regularly Update Contact Information:**
- Contact Directory: Maintain an up-to-date directory with contact information for all team members, stakeholders, and external partners. This ensures efficient communication during a crisis.

14. **Review and Update the Plan Regularly:**
- Continuous Improvement: Regularly review and update your crisis management plan based on evolving risks, lessons learned from simulations, and changes in your business environment.

15. **Educate Leadership and Employees:**
- Company-Wide Awareness: Ensure that leadership and employees are aware of the crisis management plan. Provide education on their

roles and responsibilities in supporting crisis management efforts.

16. **Secure Access to Social Media Accounts:**
- Access Control: Implement secure access controls for social media accounts. Restrict access to authorized personnel to prevent unauthorized posts during a crisis.

17. **Establish Customer Communication Channels:**
- Direct Customer Communication: Set up dedicated customer communication channels, such as a crisis hotline or email, to address customer concerns directly.

18. **Audit External Dependencies:**
- Vendor and Partner Relations: Assess the potential impact of a crisis on external dependencies, such as vendors and partners. Have contingency plans in place for critical dependencies.

19. **Understand Platform Policies:**
- Platform Compliance: Familiarize yourself with the policies and guidelines of social media platforms. Ensure that your crisis responses adhere to these guidelines to avoid additional complications.

20. **Crisis Recovery Plan:**
- Recovery Strategies: Develop a crisis recovery plan outlining strategies for rebuilding trust, restoring normal operations, and addressing the long-term impact of a crisis.

By proactively preparing for potential crises on social media, businesses can minimize the impact of unforeseen challenges and respond effectively to protect their reputation and maintain customer trust.

Swift Responses and Damage Control

Swift responses and effective damage control are critical components of crisis management on social media. Here's a guide on how to respond promptly and mitigate damage during a crisis:

1. **Acknowledge the Issue Immediately:**
   - Respond Quickly: Acknowledge the issue publicly as soon as possible. This shows your audience that you are aware of the situation and taking it seriously.

2. **Express Empathy and Apologize:**
   - Show Empathy: Express empathy for those affected by the issue. Apologize sincerely if your brand is at fault. A genuine apology can go a long way in mitigating negative sentiment.

3. **Take Responsibility:**
   - Assume Responsibility: If your brand is responsible for the issue, take ownership of it. Avoid deflection and demonstrate a commitment to resolving the problem.

4. **Provide Regular Updates:**
   - Keep the Audience Informed: Provide regular updates on the steps being taken to address the

issue. Transparency helps rebuild trust and keeps your audience informed.

5. **Designate a Spokesperson:**
- Centralized Communication: Designate a single spokesperson to communicate with the public. This ensures a consistent and controlled flow of information.

6. **Use the Right Tone:**
- Tone of Communication: Choose a tone that is appropriate for the severity of the crisis. Remain calm, professional, and empathetic in your communication.

7. **Leverage Social Media Platforms:**
- Utilize Platform Features: Use platform-specific features to address the issue. For instance, on Twitter, you can use threads for detailed explanations, and on Instagram, you can use Stories for updates.

8. **Direct Message Resolution:**

- Move Conversations Privately: Encourage individuals to move sensitive conversations to private channels, such as direct messages or customer service hotlines, to address issues more personally.

9. **Disable or Edit Inappropriate Content:**
- Control Content Visibility: If inappropriate content is spreading, consider temporarily disabling or editing the content. This helps control the spread of misinformation.

10. **Monitor and Respond to Feedback:**
- Engage with Feedback: Monitor comments and feedback on social media. Respond promptly to concerns, answer questions, and address issues raised by your audience.

11. **Implement Corrective Actions:**
- Outline Solutions: Clearly communicate the steps your brand is taking to rectify the situation. Implement corrective actions and share the progress with your audience.

12. **Seek Legal and Compliance Advice:**
- Legal Considerations: If the crisis involves legal considerations, consult with legal experts to ensure that your responses comply with regulations and mitigate legal risks.

13. **Learn from the Crisis:**
- Conduct a Post-Crisis Review: After the crisis is resolved, conduct a comprehensive review. Identify lessons learned, areas for improvement, and update crisis management protocols accordingly.

14. **Reassure Your Audience:**
- Rebuild Trust: Emphasize your commitment to resolving the issue and preventing similar incidents in the future. Reassure your audience of your dedication to their satisfaction.

15. **Highlight Positive Actions:**
- Showcase Positive Initiatives: If applicable, highlight positive actions or initiatives your

brand is taking that align with your values. This can help shift the narrative toward positive aspects.

16. **Involve Influencers or Advocates:**
- Positive Advocacy: If appropriate, involve influencers or brand advocates to support your message and reassure the audience about your commitment to resolving the issue.

17. **Review Social Media Policies:**
- Update Guidelines: Review and update your social media policies based on the crisis experience. Ensure that your guidelines are robust and can handle potential challenges.

18. **Evaluate Communication Effectiveness:**
- Assess Response Impact: Evaluate how your responses are being received by monitoring sentiment and engagement metrics. Adjust communication strategies based on audience reactions.

19. **Plan for Long-Term Reputation Recovery:**
- Long-Term Strategies: Develop long-term strategies for reputation recovery. This may include ongoing engagement, positive initiatives, and rebuilding trust over time.

20. **Communicate Lessons Learned Internally:**
- Internal Communication: Share insights and lessons learned with your internal teams. This facilitates continuous learning and preparedness for future challenges.

21. **Prepare for Potential Follow-Up Questions:**
- Anticipate Questions: Be prepared for follow-up questions and concerns. Address potential inquiries proactively to demonstrate transparency.

Swift responses and effective damage control require a well-coordinated effort, transparency, and a commitment to resolving issues. By following these steps, businesses can navigate crises on social media with agility and minimize the impact on their brand reputation.

Learning from Setbacks for Future Improvement

Learning from setbacks is a crucial aspect of continuous improvement. Here's a guide on how to leverage setbacks for future improvement:

1. **Conduct a Post-Event Analysis:**
- **Thorough Examination:** After a setback or crisis, conduct a comprehensive analysis of what happened. Examine the root causes, contributing factors, and the effectiveness of your response.

2. **Gather Feedback Internally:**
- **Team Debriefing:** Engage with your internal teams for their perspectives. Gather insights from those directly involved and those who observed the situation from different perspectives.

3. **Seek External Perspectives:**
   - **External Consultants or Experts:**
Consider seeking input from external consultants
or experts who can provide an objective view of
the situation. They may bring valuable insights
and best practices.

4. **Identify Lessons Learned:**
   - **Key Takeaways:** Distill key lessons
learned from the setback. What worked well?
What could be improved? Use these takeaways
as the foundation for future improvements.

5. **Document Findings and
Recommendations:**
   - **Comprehensive Documentation:**
Document your findings and recommendations
in a clear and comprehensive manner. This
serves as a reference for future planning and
improvements.

6. **Review and Update Protocols:**

- **Protocol Revisions:** If your crisis management plan or protocols were insufficient, revise and update them based on the lessons learned. Ensure they address potential scenarios more effectively.

7. **Implement Corrective Actions:**
- **Concrete Steps:** Implement corrective actions based on your findings. This may involve changes to processes, communication strategies, or internal procedures to prevent a similar setback in the future.

8. **Communicate Changes Internally:**
- **Internal Communication:** Clearly communicate changes and improvements to your internal teams. Ensure everyone is aware of the adjustments made to address the identified issues.

9. **Establish a Continuous Improvement Culture:**
- **Encourage Feedback:** Foster a culture that encourages open communication and

feedback. Create channels for team members to share insights and suggestions for improvement.

10. **Train Teams Based on Learnings:**
- **Targeted Training:** Provide targeted training for teams based on the lessons learned. This may involve crisis response training, communication skills development, or specific skill-building exercises.

11. **Simulate Scenarios:**
- **Scenario Simulations:** Regularly conduct scenario simulations to test your team's response to potential setbacks. This proactive approach helps reinforce learning and preparedness.

12. **Establish Key Performance Indicators (KPIs):**
- **Metrics for Improvement:** Define KPIs that reflect the effectiveness of your crisis management and improvement efforts. Regularly monitor these metrics to gauge progress.

13. **Encourage Innovation:**
- **Innovative Solutions:** Encourage team members to propose innovative solutions based on the setbacks. An environment that values innovation can lead to creative approaches to preventing similar issues.

14. **Regularly Review and Reflect:**
- **Ongoing Reflection:** Regularly review past setbacks and reflect on the progress made. Continuously refine your approach to learning from setbacks as part of an ongoing improvement process.

15. **Benchmark Against Industry Best Practices:**
- **Industry Comparisons:** Benchmark your crisis management practices against industry best practices. Identify areas where your approach can align more closely with proven successful strategies.

16. **Foster Cross-Functional Collaboration:**

- **Collaboration Across Teams:**
Encourage cross-functional collaboration.
Learning from setbacks often requires input
from various departments and perspectives.

17. **Stay Informed About Industry Trends:**
- **Industry Updates:** Stay informed about
industry trends and advancements. Adapt your
crisis management strategies to align with the
evolving landscape of your industry.

18. **Build Resilience:**
- **Resilience Training:** Build resilience
within your teams through training programs.
Resilient teams can better navigate setbacks and
emerge stronger from challenges.

19. **Celebrate Successes and Improvements:**
- **Recognition:** Acknowledge and
celebrate successes resulting from
improvements. Recognition boosts morale and

reinforces the importance of learning from setbacks.

20. **Document Success Stories:**
- **Success Case Studies:** Document success stories that resulted from the implementation of improvements. Use these case studies to inspire and motivate your teams.

21. **Iterate and Adapt:**
- **Iterative Process:** Recognize that learning from setbacks is an iterative process. Continuously iterate and adapt your approach based on ongoing experiences and feedback.

Leveraging setbacks for future improvement is a dynamic and ongoing process. By adopting a proactive and reflective approach, organizations can build resilience, enhance their crisis management capabilities, and continually evolve in the face of challenges.

Chapter 11
Measuring Success and ROI

Measuring success and return on investment (ROI) in social media involves tracking key metrics that align with your business goals. Here's a guide on how to effectively measure success and ROI on social media:

1. **Define Clear Objectives:**
- **Goal Setting:** Clearly define your social media objectives. Whether it's increasing brand awareness, driving website traffic, or generating leads, having specific goals is essential for measuring success.

2. **Identify Key Performance Indicators (KPIs):**
- **Relevant Metrics:** Choose KPIs that directly align with your objectives. Common social media KPIs include engagement rate, reach, click-through rate, conversion rate, and follower growth.

3. **Use Platform Analytics:**
- **Platform-Specific Insights:** Leverage analytics tools provided by social media platforms (e.g., Facebook Insights, Twitter Analytics, Instagram Insights) to track performance metrics. These tools offer valuable data on audience behavior and engagement.

4. **Implement UTM Parameters:**
- **Custom Tracking Links:** Use UTM parameters in your URLs to track the effectiveness of social media campaigns in Google Analytics. This helps attribute website traffic and conversions to specific social media efforts.

5. **Monitor Reach and Engagement:**
- **Audience Interaction:** Track metrics related to reach (how many people saw your content) and engagement (likes, comments, shares). High engagement often correlates with a successful social media strategy.

6. **Evaluate Conversion Metrics:**
- **Conversion Tracking:** If your goal is to drive conversions (e.g., sales, sign-ups), use conversion tracking tools. Measure the number of conversions directly attributed to your social media efforts.

7. **Calculate Cost-Per-Click (CPC) and Cost-Per-Conversion:**
- **Financial Metrics:** Calculate CPC (cost per click) and cost-per-conversion to understand the financial efficiency of your paid social media campaigns.

8. **Customer Acquisition Cost (CAC):**
- **Acquisition Expenses:** Calculate the CAC by dividing the total costs of acquiring customers through social media by the number of acquired customers. This helps assess the cost-effectiveness of your social media efforts.

9. **Measure Brand Sentiment:**
- **Sentiment Analysis:** Monitor brand sentiment through social listening tools or

manual analysis. Positive sentiment can be an indicator of successful brand perception.

10. **Track Follower Growth:**
- **Audience Growth:** Monitor the growth of your social media followers. A steady increase indicates a growing and engaged audience.

11. **Analyze Click-Through Rate (CTR):**
- **Click-Through Efficiency:** CTR measures the percentage of people who clicked on your content after seeing it. It's a valuable metric for assessing the relevance and appeal of your content.

12. **Evaluate Return on Ad Spend (ROAS):**
- **Ad Campaign Performance:** If running paid campaigns, calculate ROAS by dividing the revenue generated from ads by the cost of those ads. A ratio above 1 indicates a positive return.

13. **Social Media Listening:**
- **Conversations and Mentions:** Monitor conversations and mentions of your brand on social media. Analyze sentiment and identify areas for improvement based on feedback.

14. **Benchmark Against Industry Standards:**
- **Industry Comparisons:** Compare your social media metrics to industry benchmarks. This provides context and helps you understand how well you're performing compared to industry averages.

15. **Customer Lifetime Value (CLV):**
- **Long-Term Value:** Assess the CLV by estimating the total revenue a customer is expected to generate over their lifetime. This metric helps justify long-term social media investment.

16. **Survey and Feedback:**
- **Customer Surveys:** Collect feedback directly from your audience through surveys.

Understand their perceptions and preferences to refine your social media strategy.

17. **Attribution Models:**
- **Multi-Touch Attribution:** Implement multi-touch attribution models to understand how various touchpoints contribute to conversions. This provides insights into the customer journey influenced by social media.

18. **Regular Reporting and Analysis:**
- **Periodic Assessment:** Establish a regular reporting schedule to analyze social media performance. This ongoing analysis allows for timely adjustments and optimizations.

19. **Social Media Audit:**
- **Comprehensive Review:** Conduct periodic social media audits to assess overall performance, identify areas for improvement, and realign strategies with changing business goals.

20. **ROI Calculation:**

- **Return on Investment Formula:**
Calculate ROI by subtracting the total cost of your social media efforts from the revenue generated and dividing the result by the total cost. Multiply by 100 to express as a percentage.

21. **Iterate and Optimize:**
- **Continuous Improvement:** Use insights gained from measurements to iterate and optimize your social media strategy continually. Experiment with new approaches and tactics based on performance data.

By consistently monitoring these metrics and adapting your strategy based on insights gained, you can effectively measure success and ROI on social media. Remember that social media success is often a dynamic and evolving process, and ongoing refinement is key to sustained performance.

Defining Key Performance Indicators (KPIs)

Defining key performance indicators (KPIs) is crucial for assessing the success of your social media strategy. Here's a guide on how to identify relevant KPIs based on your business objectives:

1. **Brand Awareness:**
- **KPI:** **Reach and Impressions**
- **Rationale:** Measure the number of people who see your content (reach) and how often it's seen (impressions) to gauge the overall awareness of your brand.

2. **Audience Engagement:**
- **KPI:** **Engagement Rate (Likes, Comments, Shares)**
- **Rationale:** Evaluate how well your audience interacts with your content. Higher engagement rates indicate that your content resonates with your audience.

3. **Website Traffic:**
- **KPI:** **Click-Through Rate (CTR)**
- **Rationale:** Track the percentage of users who click on your social media content and visit

your website. A higher CTR signifies effective content driving traffic.

4. **Lead Generation:**
- **KPI:** **Conversion Rate**
- **Rationale:** Measure the rate at which social media leads convert into desired actions, such as sign-ups or downloads. A higher conversion rate indicates effective lead generation.

5. **Customer Acquisition:**
- **KPI:** **Cost per Acquisition (CPA)**
- **Rationale:** Calculate the cost of acquiring a customer through social media advertising. A lower CPA suggests efficient customer acquisition.

6. **Follower Growth:**
- **KPI:** **Follower Growth Rate**
- **Rationale:** Track the rate at which your social media following is expanding. Consistent growth indicates increasing brand reach and influence.

7. **Customer Retention:**
- **KPI:** **Customer Satisfaction Score (CSAT)**
- **Rationale:** Assess customer satisfaction by soliciting feedback. A high CSAT suggests satisfied customers likely to stay loyal.

8. **Community Engagement:**
- **KPI:** **Community Participation (Discussions, UGC)**
- **Rationale:** Measure the level of engagement within your community, including discussions and user-generated content. Strong community participation fosters brand loyalty.

9. **Influence and Thought Leadership:**
- **KPI:** **Share of Voice**
- **Rationale:** Assess your brand's share of the overall conversation within your industry on social media. A higher share of voice indicates influence and thought leadership.

10. **Content Effectiveness:**

- **KPI:** **Click-Through Rate (CTR) by Content Type**
   - **Rationale:** Analyze which types of content (e.g., videos, images, articles) drive the highest CTR. Adjust your content strategy based on effectiveness.

11. **Social Listening:**
   - **KPI:** **Sentiment Analysis**
   - **Rationale:** Monitor sentiment around your brand. Positive sentiment indicates a favorable perception, while negative sentiment signals potential issues.

12. **Employee Advocacy:**
   - **KPI:** **Employee Engagement and Advocacy**
   - **Rationale:** Measure the level of engagement and advocacy among your employees on social media. Employees sharing positive content can enhance brand credibility.

13. **Customer Lifetime Value (CLV):**

- **KPI:** **Lifetime Value of Social Media-Acquired Customers**
- **Rationale:** Assess the long-term value of customers acquired through social media efforts. Higher CLV signifies a more valuable customer base.

14. **Competitor Benchmarking:**
- **KPI:** **Competitor Comparison (Engagement, Follower Growth)**
- **Rationale:** Compare your social media performance with competitors. Benchmarking provides insights into your relative standing within the industry.

15. **Social Media Ad Effectiveness:**
- **KPI:** **Return on Ad Spend (ROAS)**
- **Rationale:** Evaluate the performance of paid social media campaigns by measuring the revenue generated compared to the ad spend.

16. **Customer Feedback and Reviews:**
- **KPI:** **Number of Positive/Negative Reviews**

- **Rationale:** Track the number and sentiment of customer reviews on social media platforms. Positive reviews contribute to brand reputation.

17. **Geographic Reach:**
- **KPI:** **Geographic Distribution of Audience**
- **Rationale:** Analyze where your social media audience is located. This insight helps tailor content and campaigns to specific geographic regions.

18. **Cross-Platform Performance:**
- **KPI:** **Cross-Platform Engagement and Conversions**
- **Rationale:** Evaluate how your social media strategy performs across different platforms. Adjust strategies based on the unique dynamics of each platform.

19. **Conversion Funnel Analysis:**
- **KPI:** **Conversion Rates at Each Funnel Stage**

- **Rationale:** Assess the efficiency of your social media efforts at each stage of the conversion funnel, from awareness to conversion.

20. **Influencer Collaboration Impact:**
   - **KPI:** **Influencer-Generated Engagement and Conversions**
   - **Rationale:** Measure the impact of influencer collaborations by tracking engagement and conversions generated through influencer-driven content.

21. **Sustainability and Social Impact:**
   - **KPI:** **Social Responsibility Metrics (e.g., Carbon Offsetting, Charitable Contributions)**
   - **Rationale:** Track and communicate social and environmental impact metrics, aligning with corporate sustainability goals.

Evaluating Social Media ROI

Evaluating social media return on investment (ROI) involves analyzing the effectiveness of your social media efforts in generating measurable outcomes. Here's a guide on how to evaluate social media ROI:

1. **Establish Clear Objectives:**
- Clearly define your social media objectives, whether they're focused on brand awareness, lead generation, sales, or other specific goals.

2. **Align Metrics with Objectives:**
- Ensure that the metrics you track align directly with your established objectives. Different goals may require different key performance indicators (KPIs).

3. **Attribution Modeling:**
- Implement attribution models to understand how different touchpoints contribute to conversions. This helps attribute value to each stage of the customer journey influenced by social media.

4. **Conversion Tracking:**
- Set up conversion tracking to monitor the actions users take after engaging with your social media content. This could include form submissions, purchases, or other desired outcomes.

5. **Use UTM Parameters:**
- Employ UTM parameters in your URLs for tracking campaign performance in Google Analytics. This allows you to attribute website traffic and conversions specifically to your social media efforts.

6. **Customer Lifetime Value (CLV):**
- Evaluate the CLV of customers acquired through social media channels. Understanding the long-term value helps justify ongoing social media investment.

7. **Calculate Cost per Acquisition (CPA):**
- Determine the cost of acquiring a customer through social media by dividing total costs by

the number of acquired customers. A lower CPA
suggests cost-effective customer acquisition.

8. **Compare Paid vs. Organic Performance:**
- Analyze the performance of paid social media efforts compared to organic activities. Assess whether the investment in paid campaigns delivers a measurable return.

9. **Social Media Ad Spend vs. Revenue:**
- Calculate the return on ad spend (ROAS) by dividing the revenue generated from social media ads by the cost of those ads. A ROAS above 1 indicates a positive return.

10. **Incrementality Testing:**
- Conduct incrementality testing to measure the true impact of your social media campaigns. This involves comparing outcomes between audiences exposed to ads and those not exposed.

11. **Assess Customer Acquisition Funnel:**
- Analyze the efficiency of your social media efforts at each stage of the customer acquisition funnel. Identify areas where improvements can lead to better outcomes.

12. **Attribution Windows:**
- Consider different attribution windows to understand the timeframe in which social media interactions contribute to conversions. Shorter or longer attribution windows may be more appropriate based on your business model.

13. **Customer Segmentation:**
- Segment your audience to analyze how different customer segments contribute to revenue. This insight can guide targeted marketing efforts.

14. **Social Media Listening:**
- Leverage social media listening tools to monitor conversations and sentiments. Analyze

how positive or negative sentiment correlates
with business outcomes.

15. **Survey and Feedback:**
- Collect feedback from customers through
surveys. Understand how social media
interactions influence their perception and
decision-making.

16. **Evaluate Influencer Collaboration
Impact:**
- Measure the impact of influencer
collaborations by assessing engagement,
conversions, and overall brand sentiment
generated through influencer-driven content.

17. **Cost-Effectiveness Across
Platforms:**
- Compare the cost-effectiveness of your
social media efforts across different platforms.
Allocate resources based on the platforms
delivering the best ROI.

18. **Benchmark Against Industry Standards:**
- Benchmark your social media ROI against industry standards to assess your performance relative to competitors and industry averages.

19. **Monitor Social Media Trends:**
- Stay informed about emerging trends in social media and adjust your strategy to leverage new opportunities that align with your business objectives.

20. **Iterative Analysis and Optimization:**
- Continuously analyze social media performance and optimize your strategy based on insights gained. Regular adjustments ensure ongoing improvement and adaptability.

21. **Qualitative Evaluation:**
- Incorporate qualitative aspects such as brand perception, customer sentiment, and overall brand equity into your evaluation. Qualitative

factors contribute to the holistic understanding of social media ROI.

22. **Review Cost Efficiency:**
- Regularly review the efficiency of your social media spending. Ensure that your budget allocation aligns with channels and activities delivering the best return.

By adopting a comprehensive approach that combines quantitative and qualitative analysis, businesses can effectively evaluate social media ROI and make informed decisions to enhance overall performance.

Adjusting Strategies for Optimal Results

Adjusting social media strategies for optimal results involves ongoing analysis, adaptation, and refinement. Here's a guide on how to adjust your strategies effectively:

1. **Regular Performance Reviews:**

- Conduct regular reviews of social media performance, analyzing key metrics and KPIs to identify trends and areas for improvement.

2. **Customer Feedback Analysis:**
- Analyze customer feedback and comments on social media platforms. Use insights gained to refine content, address concerns, and enhance engagement.

3. **Competitor Benchmarking:**
- Continuously benchmark your social media performance against competitors. Identify successful strategies and areas where you can differentiate.

4. **Platform-Specific Optimization:**
- Optimize content for each social media platform based on its unique dynamics. Tailor content formats, messaging, and posting schedules to align with platform preferences.

5. **A/B Testing:**

- Implement A/B testing for various elements such as ad copy, visuals, and posting times. Analyze the results to identify the most effective variations.

6. **Content Calendar Adjustments:**
- Adjust your content calendar based on performance data. Prioritize content types and topics that resonate with your audience and contribute to your goals.

7. **Explore New Content Formats:**
- Experiment with new content formats, such as video, live streams, or interactive content. Stay abreast of trends and incorporate innovative approaches to keep your content fresh.

8. **Segmented Audience Targeting:**
- Refine audience segments based on performance data. Tailor content and ad targeting to specific audience segments for more personalized and effective communication.

9. **Ad Spend Allocation:**

- Reevaluate your ad spend allocation across different platforms and campaigns. Shift budget towards channels delivering the best ROI and adjust bids based on performance.

10. **Geo-Targeting Optimization:**
- Optimize geo-targeting settings for specific campaigns. Tailor content and promotions to resonate with the preferences and behaviors of audiences in different locations.

11. **Influencer Collaboration Adjustments:**
- Assess the impact of influencer collaborations and adjust strategies based on performance metrics. Consider collaborating with influencers who align more closely with your brand and audience.

12. **Reassess Posting Frequency:**
- Reevaluate your posting frequency. Adjust the number of posts based on audience engagement patterns and platform algorithms to avoid content fatigue.

13. **Embrace Trending Topics:**
- Incorporate trending topics and hashtags that align with your brand. Capitalize on popular conversations to enhance visibility and engagement.

14. **Customer Persona Refinement:**
- Refine customer personas based on evolving audience behaviors and preferences. Ensure that your content strategy speaks directly to the interests of your target audience.

15. **Collaborate with Analytics Teams:**
- Collaborate with analytics teams to gain deeper insights into data trends. Utilize advanced analytics tools and techniques for more sophisticated analysis.

16. **Employee Advocacy Program Enhancements:**
- Enhance your employee advocacy program based on employee feedback and engagement

data. Encourage employees to share content and participate in brand advocacy.

17. **Community Engagement Strategies:**
- Adjust community engagement strategies based on community feedback and participation. Foster a positive and interactive community environment.

18. **Storytelling Evolution:**
- Evolve your storytelling approach. Incorporate customer testimonials, success stories, and behind-the-scenes content to create a compelling narrative.

19. **Mobile Optimization:**
- Optimize content and campaigns for mobile users. With the majority of social media users accessing platforms via mobile devices, ensure a seamless mobile experience.

20. **Evaluate Response Strategies:**

- Evaluate how your brand responds to comments, messages, and feedback. Adjust response strategies to maintain a positive and responsive online presence.

21. **Adapt to Algorithm Changes:**
- Stay informed about changes in social media algorithms. Adjust your strategy to align with algorithm updates and capitalize on new features introduced by platforms.

22. **Diversify Content Sources:**
- Diversify the sources of your content. Encourage user-generated content, collaborate with influencers, and incorporate diverse perspectives to enrich your content strategy.

23. **Continuous Learning and Training:**
- Foster a culture of continuous learning among your social media teams. Provide ongoing training to stay updated on industry trends and best practices.

24. **Evaluate Crisis Response Protocols:**
- Periodically review and update crisis response protocols. Ensure that your team is well-prepared to handle unexpected challenges and crises effectively.

25. **Strategic Partnerships:**
- Explore strategic partnerships with other brands or organizations. Collaborate on joint campaigns or initiatives to expand reach and tap into new audiences.

By adopting a proactive approach to analysis and adaptation, businesses can optimize their social media strategies for sustained success and ensure that their efforts remain aligned with evolving audience expectations and industry trends.

Chapter 12

Conclusion

In conclusion, navigating the dynamic landscape of social media for business success requires a strategic and adaptive approach. The journey from defining business objectives to evaluating ROI is a continuous loop of analysis, refinement, and innovation. Here's a recap of key takeaways:

1. **Clear Objectives Drive Strategy:**
- Start by defining clear and measurable objectives aligned with your business goals. Whether it's brand awareness, lead generation, or sales, having a clear purpose guides your social media strategy.

2. **Strategic Planning and Execution:**
- Develop a comprehensive social media strategy that encompasses content creation, audience engagement, and paid advertising. Execute this strategy consistently to build a strong and sustainable online presence.

3. **Audience Understanding is Key:**

- Invest time in understanding your audience through demographic analysis and behavioral insights. Tailor your content and engagement strategies to resonate with the preferences and interests of your target audience.

4. **Data-Driven Decision-Making:**
- Regularly analyze performance metrics and KPIs to make informed decisions. Utilize data to identify trends, measure success, and pinpoint areas for improvement.

5. **Flexibility and Adaptability:**
- Social media is dynamic; be ready to adapt. Adjust your strategies based on changing algorithms, audience behaviors, and emerging trends. Flexibility is essential for staying ahead in the ever-evolving digital landscape.

6. **Continuous Improvement Loop:**
- Establish a continuous improvement loop. Learn from setbacks, refine strategies, and iterate based on insights gained. Embrace a culture of learning and adaptation.

7. **Measuring ROI for Accountability:**
- Measure the success and ROI of your social media efforts to ensure accountability. Align metrics with business objectives, track performance, and adjust strategies accordingly.

8. **Engagement and Community Building:**
- Prioritize engagement and community building. Foster meaningful connections with your audience, encourage user-generated content, and create a positive online community around your brand.

9. **Content Innovation and Diversity:**
- Innovate your content strategy by experimenting with new formats and storytelling techniques. Diversify content sources, collaborate with influencers, and leverage user-generated content to keep your content fresh and engaging.

10. **Crisis Preparedness:**

- Be prepared for potential crises by having robust crisis management protocols in place. Respond swiftly, transparently, and empathetically to address issues and maintain trust with your audience.

11. **Ongoing Learning and Adaptation:**
   - Stay informed about industry trends, platform changes, and emerging technologies. Foster a culture of continuous learning within your team to adapt to the evolving social media landscape.

12. **Strategic Partnerships and Collaborations:**
   - Explore strategic partnerships and collaborations with other brands or influencers. Joint campaigns and initiatives can amplify your reach and introduce your brand to new audiences.

By integrating these principles into your social media approach, you can create a resilient, adaptive, and effective strategy that not only meets your business objectives but also builds a strong and enduring connection with your audience in the ever-evolving digital realm. Social media success is not just about the destination; it's about the journey of continuous improvement and innovation.

Recap of Key Strategies

Certainly! Let's recap the key strategies for social media success:

1. **Define Clear Objectives:**
- Establish specific and measurable objectives that align with your overall business goals. Whether it's brand awareness, lead generation, or sales, clear objectives provide a foundation for your social media strategy.

2. **Strategic Planning and Execution:**
- Develop a comprehensive social media strategy that encompasses content creation, audience engagement, and paid advertising.

Execute your strategy consistently to establish a strong and sustainable online presence.

3. **Audience Understanding:**
- Invest time in understanding your audience through demographic analysis and behavioral insights. Tailor your content and engagement strategies to resonate with the preferences and interests of your target audience.

4. **Data-Driven Decision-Making:**
- Regularly analyze performance metrics and key performance indicators (KPIs) to make informed decisions. Use data to identify trends, measure success, and pinpoint areas for improvement.

5. **Flexibility and Adaptability:**
- Stay flexible and adaptable to changes in algorithms, audience behaviors, and emerging trends. Adjust your strategies to remain relevant and effective in the dynamic social media landscape.

6. **Continuous Improvement Loop:**
- Establish a continuous improvement loop. Learn from setbacks, refine strategies, and iterate based on insights gained. Embrace a culture of learning and adaptation for sustained success.

7. **Measuring ROI for Accountability:**
- Measure the success and return on investment (ROI) of your social media efforts. Align metrics with business objectives, track performance, and adjust strategies to optimize results and ensure accountability.

8. **Engagement and Community Building:**
- Prioritize engagement and community building. Foster meaningful connections with your audience, encourage user-generated content, and create a positive online community around your brand.

9. **Content Innovation and Diversity:**

- Innovate your content strategy by experimenting with new formats and storytelling techniques. Diversify content sources, collaborate with influencers, and leverage user-generated content to keep your content fresh and engaging.

10. **Crisis Preparedness:**
- Be prepared for potential crises by having robust crisis management protocols in place. Respond swiftly, transparently, and empathetically to address issues and maintain trust with your audience.

11. **Ongoing Learning and Adaptation:**
- Stay informed about industry trends, platform changes, and emerging technologies. Foster a culture of continuous learning within your team to adapt to the evolving social media landscape.

12. **Strategic Partnerships and Collaborations:**

- Explore strategic partnerships and collaborations with other brands or influencers. Joint campaigns and initiatives can amplify your reach and introduce your brand to new audiences.

By integrating these key strategies into your social media approach, you can build a resilient and effective strategy that not only meets your business objectives but also creates a lasting impact in the ever-changing world of social media.

Looking Ahead: Evolving with Social Media Trends

Looking ahead, evolving with social media trends is crucial to maintaining relevance and harnessing new opportunities. Here's a guide on how to stay ahead and adapt to emerging trends:

1. **Stay Informed on Emerging Platforms:**

- Keep a pulse on emerging social media platforms. Explore and assess their relevance to your target audience. Early adoption can provide a competitive advantage.

2. **Video Dominance:**
- Embrace the dominance of video content. Invest in creating engaging and high-quality videos, including live streams and short-form videos, to capture audience attention.

3. **Augmented Reality (AR) and Virtual Reality (VR):**
- Explore the potential of AR and VR technologies for immersive brand experiences. Implement AR filters, virtual try-ons, or interactive VR content to enhance user engagement.

4. **Ephemeral Content:**
- Leverage ephemeral content, such as Stories on platforms like Instagram and Snapchat. These temporary posts create a sense of urgency and authenticity, fostering real-time connections.

5. **Social Commerce Integration:**
   - Integrate social commerce features to facilitate seamless shopping experiences directly on social media platforms. Utilize in-app purchasing, shoppable posts, and checkout functionalities.

6. **User-Generated Content (UGC) Continuation:**
   - Continue encouraging user-generated content. UGC builds community, authenticity, and trust. Implement branded challenges, hashtags, and contests to inspire user participation.

7. **Chatbots and Messaging Apps:**
   - Embrace chatbots and messaging apps for personalized customer interactions. Automate responses, provide instant support, and enhance the overall user experience.

8. **Inclusive and Diverse Content:**

- Prioritize inclusive and diverse content. Reflect a variety of voices and perspectives in your content to resonate with a broader audience and align with societal values.

9. **Interactive Content Formats:**
- Experiment with interactive content formats like polls, quizzes, and interactive infographics. Engagement increases when users actively participate in content.

10. **Micro-Influencers and Niche Communities:**
- Consider collaborating with micro-influencers and engaging with niche communities. These influencers often have highly engaged, specific audiences that align with your brand.

11. **Cross-Platform Integration:**
- Integrate your social media efforts across platforms for a cohesive brand presence. Ensure a consistent message while tailoring content to each platform's unique audience.

12. **Purpose-Driven Marketing:**
   - Emphasize purpose-driven marketing. Consumers appreciate brands that stand for social and environmental causes. Align your brand with meaningful initiatives.

13. **Short-Form Content Optimization:**
   - Optimize for short-form content consumption. Short attention spans mean concise and impactful messaging is crucial. Platforms like TikTok exemplify the popularity of bite-sized content.

14. **Podcasting and Audio Content:**
   - Explore the growth of podcasts and audio content. Develop podcasts or participate in audio spaces to reach audiences who prefer consuming content through audio channels.

15. **Data Privacy and Transparency:**
   - Prioritize data privacy and transparency. Communicate clearly about how user data is

handled, building trust and aligning with evolving privacy expectations.

16. **NFTs and Digital Collectibles:**
- Stay attuned to the rise of NFTs (Non-Fungible Tokens) and digital collectibles. Evaluate how these digital assets can be incorporated into your brand strategy.

17. **Gamification Strategies:**
- Implement gamification elements in your social media strategy. Games, challenges, and interactive features can enhance user engagement and create memorable experiences.

18. **Voice Search Optimization:**
- Optimize content for voice search. As voice-activated devices become more prevalent, ensure your content is discoverable through voice searches on platforms like Amazon Alexa or Google Assistant.

19. **Social Responsibility and Sustainability:**

- Emphasize social responsibility and sustainability in your brand narrative. Consumers increasingly support brands that actively contribute to positive social and environmental impact.

20. **Algorithm Adaptation:**
- Stay agile in adapting to changes in social media algorithms. Regularly monitor updates from platforms and adjust your content strategy accordingly.

21. **Humanize Your Brand:**
- Humanize your brand by showcasing behind-the-scenes content, employee stories, and authentic moments. Build a connection with your audience beyond the products or services you offer.

22. **Education and Information Sharing:**
- Position your brand as an educational resource. Share informative content, tutorials, and industry insights to establish authority and provide value to your audience.

By proactively embracing these evolving trends, your business can stay ahead of the curve, connect with audiences in meaningful ways, and continually adapt to the ever-changing landscape of social media.